Brave Old Man	Yellow Wolf	Wears Hat On Side
Bull Child	White Weasel	Night Walker
Buck Medicine	Double Gun	Old Rock
Spotted Eagle	Gambler	Old Kayote
Heavy Runner	Lone Medicine Man	Broad Back
E-co-me	Red Eagle	The Lone Man
Bear Shoes	Red Head	White Man
Feather Tail Chief	Black Bear	Big Spring
Berry Carrier	Owl Medicine	Wolf Eagle
Lone Star	Weasel Horn	Grebs
Man Loves Tobacco	Ear Ring	Brain Head
Batiste Roundin	Wolf Shoe	Bad Old Man
Last Star	Cow Running On Side Hill	White Antelope
Eagle Head	Buck Chief	Chief Crow
Black Cayote	Crow Feather	Temporary Married
Antelope Running	Crow Gut	Bones
Big Road	Running Crane Three	Young Crow
Lone Horn	Under Bull	Chief Standing Alone
Chief Elk	Red Plume	Bull Medicine
Bird Flies	Scably	Mexican
Poor Eagle	Good Warrior	Red Paint
Good Shield	Cree Medicine	Man Who Don't Run
Lone Chief	Eagle Rib	Bear Leggings
Hairy Coat	Lodge Pole Chief	Small Robe
Morning Eagle	Medicine Weasel	Big Pole
Man Shoot In Air	Morning Plume	Man Don't Go Out
Small Bear	Sharp	Man Takes Plenty Arms
Man Sits From Them	Take Gun From Both Sides	Man Holds Pipe
Black Foot Child	Man Rides Horse In A Day	Top Chief
Bull's Son	Coat	Iron Gun Taker
Black Sousee	Side and Side	Pities People
Heavy Gun	White Cow Looking	Night Gunman
Eagle	About To Shoot	Running Fisher
Second Lone Chief	Tail Feathers	Plenty Bears
Eagle Talk	Two Fox	Wolf Child
Split Ear	Last Shot	Mean Drinker
Wolfverine	Arrow Top	

NO MORE
BUFFALO

This book is dedicated to
Neetsee-tahpee, the Blackfeet.
A people who have lived a glorious past
and who now look forward to an enlightened future.

NO MORE

BY BOB SCRIVER

with the assistance of
Dr. Harold McCracken, Dr. John C. Ew

BUFFALO

...holas deVore III, Marshall Noice & Carl Cree Medicine   The Lowell Press / Kansas City

PHOTO CREDITS: Nicholas deVore III, pages viii, 2, 4, 16, 20, 23, 24, 31, 56, 58, 63, 70, 76, 78, 94, 108, 116, 126 bottom, dustjacket front; C. J. Henry, page 22; Jim Krieg, page 121; Karen Jo Nelson, page 126 top; Marshall Noice, pages 6, 8, 12, 15, 30, 32, 34, 37, 40, 41, 42, 44, 46, 48, 50, 57, 59, 62, 64, 68, 74, 80, 82, 86, 88, 90, 92, 96, 98, 102, 104, 110, 114, 124, 125, 126 middle, dustjacket back; Mel Ruder, page 33; Bob Scriver, pages ii, xviii, 6, 26, 53, 54, 60, 61, 88, 90, 106, 110, 123.

Library of Congress Cataloging in Publication Data

Scriver, Bob, 1914—
No more buffalo.

Bibliography: p.
1. Siksika Indians—History.
2. Siksika Indians—Sculpture.
3. Indians of North America—Great Plains—Sculpture.
I. Title.
E99.S54S36   970.004'97   82-15194
ISBN 0-913504-75-0   AACR2

The paper in this book meets the guidelines for permanence and durability of the Committee on Production Guidelines for Book Longevity of the Council on Library Resources.

FIRST EDITION

Printed in the United States of America by The Lowell Press, Inc., Kansas City, Missouri

BOB SCRIVER

Sik-Poke-Sah-Ma-Pee

I have known Bob Scriver for many years; in fact, he was my high school band instructor. I played in his championship bands along with Bill Byrne, now with the Woody Herman Orchestra in New York City.

Bob was well-acquainted with my parents and has always lived here among the Blackfeet where he is known and respected by them. His family was also one of the first to establish a business here on the reservation.

In 1970, the Blackfeet granted him the privilege of becoming the owner of a sacred Medicine Pipe. This pipe was transferred to him in the old way in a ceremony that was authentic in every detail. No higher honor can be bestowed upon anyone by the Blackfeet. The name given to him at the time of the transfer of the pipe was Sik-Poke-Sah-Ma-Pee, the name of a famous warrior of the olden times.

Bob Scriver's sympathetic understanding of my people is remarkably shown in these sculptures. Sik-Poke-Sah-Ma-Pee has the wholehearted support of both myself and my people. We are proud to call him one of us and are proud that he has chosen us as the subject for this work.

Earl Old Person, Chairman
Blackfeet Tribal Business Council

Hereditary Chief of the Pikuni

Past President of National Congress
of American Indians

To Carol and Keith Johnston

Please have good memories of Browning — home of The Blackfeet — Best wishes

Bob Scriver

83

The
Personal Library
of

Donald Johnston

CONTENTS

PREFACE
Creation of the Blackfeet Series

In 1959, Meade Swingley, Chairman of the Blackfeet Tribal Business Council, approached me with an idea. He and the Council wished to commission me to create a series of twelve statues of larger than life-size proportions depicting various facets of the Blackfeet culture. I thought it a great idea so I immediately got to work: "No More Buffalo," "Return of the Blackfeet Raiders," "Coming of Elk-Dog," "Life's Stream," and "Transition" were among the first of these sculptures. They were all done in small scale to await the foundry enlarging process. Meade Swingley met an untimely death due to a deadly virus, and without his aggressive leadership the project came to a halt. For many years I dreamt of continuing this project so I kept on developing ideas as they came to me.

Instead of twelve heroic-size statues, my attention turned to a series of much larger scope depicting a wide range of subjects, including religion, recreation, war, mythology, family life and more in the historical period from about 750 A.D. to 1950 A.D. In the initial concept for a series of this magnitude there were 97 ideas, but realizing that 97 pieces would become too large and unwieldy, I reduced the number to 53, which I feel is minimal in telling the story covering 1,200 years of a people's culture.

The series begins with the primeval Blackfeet man and ends with "Transition." Sad it is to witness this dying culture of the Blackfeet, but their original free society is diametrically opposed to the regimentation of today's social order. In the purest sense the two societies have irreconcilable differences at the most basic levels—religious beliefs, concepts of ownership and true independence of the individual.

The Blackfeet have survived three rapid, major cultural upheavals of their stone age society. Some of the Blackfeet living today have known the horse age, the auto age and the space age with satellite pictures of man walking on the surface of Night Light (the moon). All of these great changes have taken place in the past two hundred years, a period of time which spans only ten generations.

Many of the younger people of Blackfeet ancestry are showing an increased interest in the ways of the ancient ones and are finding ways to weld the two societies together so that the people are not torn between having to live one way or the other but rather are striving to combine the best of both.

Respectfully submitted
to all people and especially
Neetsee-tahpee
Un-Yuh (I have spoken).

Sik-Poke-Sah-Ma-Pee
Bob Scriver
June 1982

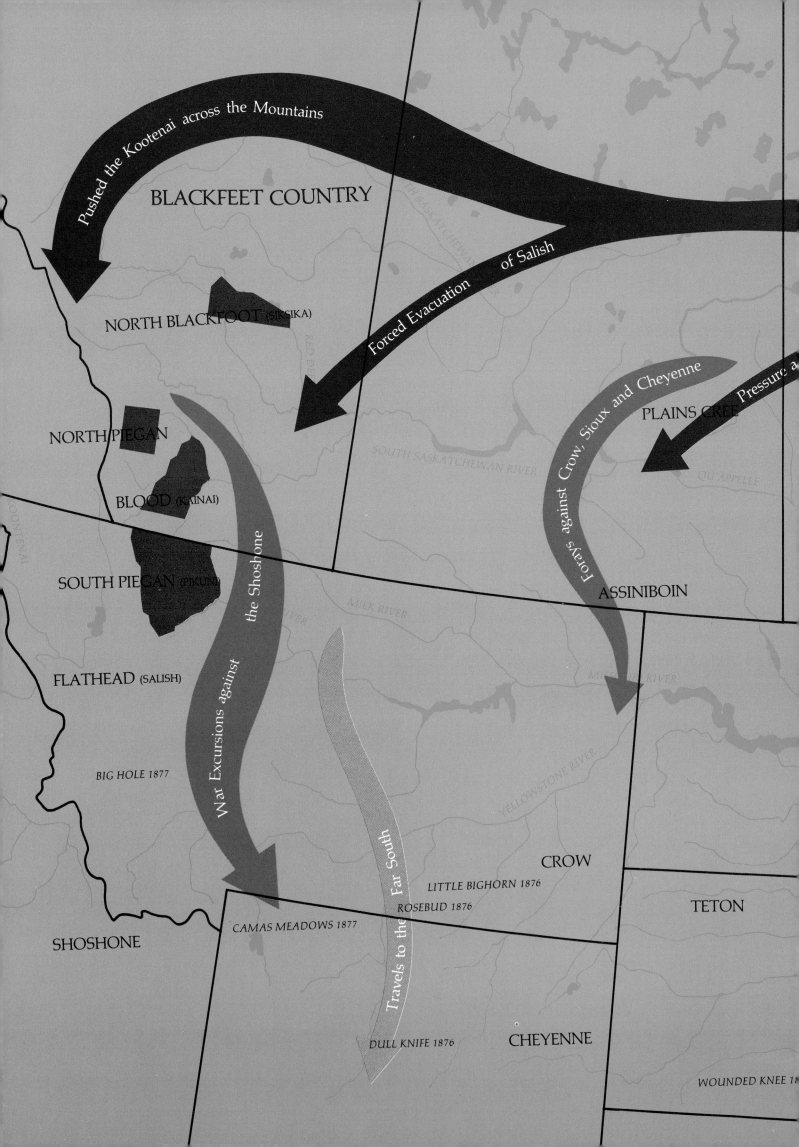

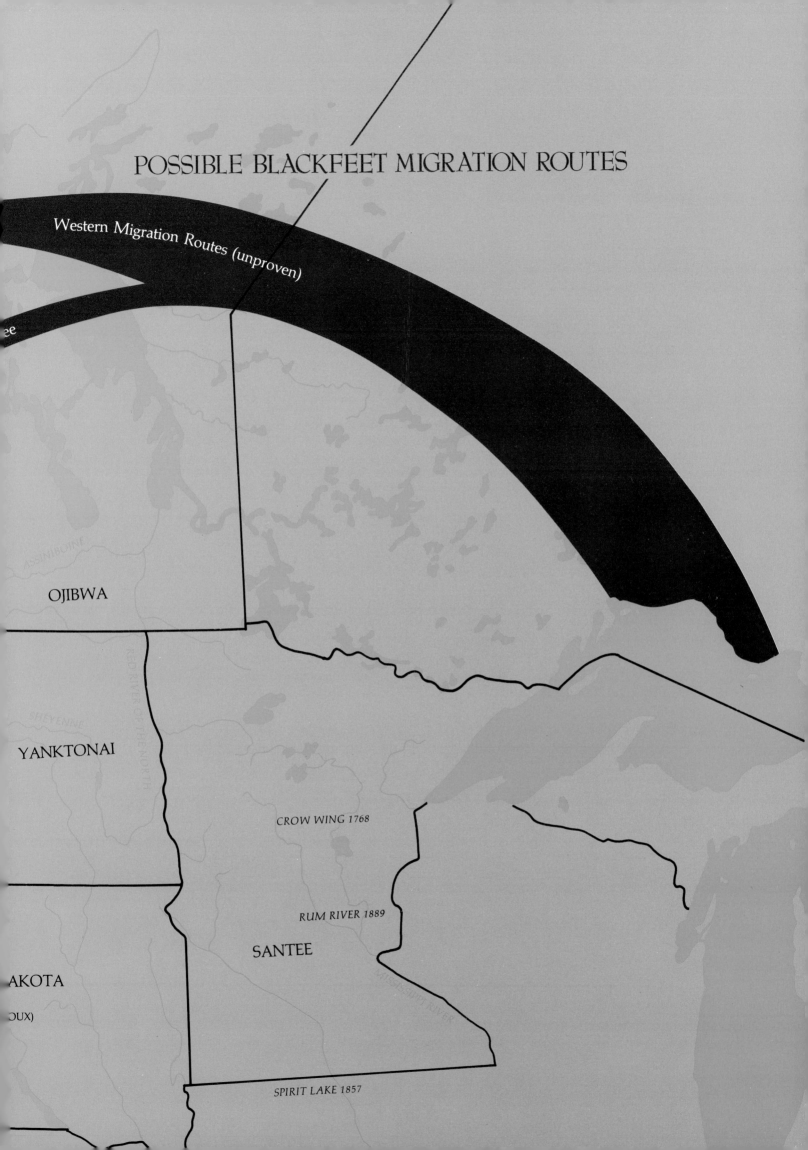

POSSIBLE BLACKFEET MIGRATION ROUTES

Western Migration Routes (unproven)

ee

ASSINIBOINE

OJIBWA

RED RIVER OF THE NORTH

SHEYENNE

YANKTONAI

CROW WING 1768

RUM RIVER 1889

SANTEE

MISSISSIPPI RIVER

AKOTA

OUX)

SPIRIT LAKE 1857

ACKNOWLEDGMENTS

I regret that I can list the names of only some of the many people who have given of their time and talents to help make this volume become a reality. I acknowledge and thank the following for their special contributions to *No More Buffalo:*

Doug Chadwick, Phil Scriver and Bert Gildart who acted as manuscript advisors; Nicholas deVore III and Marshall Noice, the principal photographers; Steve Ard who offered photo and technical assistance; Jim Scriver and Joseph Red Fox for technical assistance; Iola Brenneman, Marie Caldwell and Connie McKnight, manuscript typists; Amy Pannoni who critiqued and typed the final manuscript;

Tom Troy, artistic critiques of the sculpture; Diane Melting Tallow, Adolf and Beverly Hungry Wolf, Tom, Alice and Danny Kehoe of the Milwaukee Public Museum for anthropological information; Hugh Dempsey, anthropologist of the Glenbow Museum in Calgary, Alberta, and Ted Brasser of Ottawa National Museum for ethnological information; Wilbur P. Werner for recording the pedigree of the Badger Tipi;

Big Horn Foundry, Powell Foundry and Kalispell Art Casting for painstaking attention to detail in the casting process;

Mr. C. J. Henry, manager, National Bison Range, Moiese, Montana; Victor May, range foreman, National Bison Range, and Ernie Kraft for help with the buffalo sequences; Mr. Eric Harvie; Mr. Hod Meech and Mr. Harry Critchley of the Riveredge Foundation, Calgary, Alberta for moral and financial support;

Dr. Harold McCracken and Dr. John C. Ewers for encouragement and support; Carl Cree Medicine who was my major language consultant and a technical master; George and Molly Kicking Woman for giving me an insight into Blackfeet spiritual matters; Dr. and Mrs. E. L. King for help and encouragement; Meade Swingley, Earl Old Person and the Blackfeet Tribal Council along with all my Blackfeet friends here and in Canada for encouragement and support;

My personal friends John Clymer, Robert E. Lougheed, Tom Lovell, Bob Kuhn, Marquita Maytag and Bill Cochran for encouragement and support; Roberta Whitcomb, manuscript critique, and Ruth Hill for much friendly advice; Mary Scriver, Mix-skim-ee-ah-kee (Iron Woman); Helene DeVicq and Maurice Caouette for encouragement, artistic advice and support; Cecile Mountain Chief Horn, my friend, for advice and information on things concerning the Blackfeet; Payson W. Lowell, Barbara Funk and Dave Spaw, together with all the employees of The Lowell Press, for bringing this book into being; Ray W. Steele, director of the C. M. Russell Museum in Great Falls, for his aid, encouragement and advice in arranging the world premier of this series of sculptures;

And my wife, Lorraine, who got her Blackfeet name Me-sin-skee-ah-kee (Badger Woman) at our annual pipe opening, has given me encouragement, moral support and helpful suggestions and was a staunch partner throughout this venture.

FOREWORD
by Dr. Harold McCracken

Director Emeritus
Whitney Gallery of Western Art
Cody, Wyoming

A truly extraordinary man, Dr. Harold McCracken is an individual of many talents and varied interests: aviator, writer, lecturer, naturalist, archaeologist, anthropologist and ethnologist. Dr. McCracken was invited to be an honored guest of the Blackfeet when I became the recipient of the Little Dog Medicine Pipe, so, having viewed this ancient ritual firsthand, Dr. McCracken is well qualified to write a few words attesting to the authenticity of this book.

For his studies of the Alaskan brown bear, the University of Alaska granted him an honorary doctorate. He has also been awarded four other honorary doctorates and is the author of thirty-one books. I am deeply indebted to Dr. Harold McCracken for all he has done for me, both as a friend and patron. —R.M.S.

NO MORE BUFFALO

Preservation of Blackfeet History in Bronze and Text

Bob Scriver is a dedicated historian of the Blackfeet Indians; and his thesis in everlasting bronze accompanied by his authoritative text is unique in the field of Western American art as well as any of our Indian tribes. This book and its assemblage of fine photographs is a conspicuous consummation of that fact.

Born August 15, 1914, in Browning, Montana, the tribal metropolis of the Blackfeet on their large reservation in northwestern Montana, Robert Macfie Scriver has always made his home among these traditionally classic native people. His father, Thaddeus Emery Scriver, who was of original pioneer stock from eastern Canada, came to Browning in 1900 where he started the Browning Mercantile Company for trading with the Blackfeet Indians and supplying them with credit and the white man's necessities for a transition from the primitive to a more modern way of

life. Thus, Bob grew up with Blackfeet friends, completing his grade school and high school education there, graduating from high school as valedictorian of his class.

Bob's first serious interest was music, which motivated him to attend the VanderCook College of Music in Chicago where he acquired a Bachelor's Degree in 1935 and a Master's Degree in 1941. He played his cornet with Ted Weems' orchestra.

But he kept coming back to his home on the Blackfeet Indian Reservation and in 1951 settled down to make Browning his permanent home. Always having been interested in natural history and big game hunting, which abounded in the region, circumstances led him into the taxidermy business. As an adjunct to this, he developed a small museum for which he created a series of dioramas of miniature polychromed figures of animals as well as Blackfeet Indians. It was the latter that led Bob Scriver into his singular thesis of preserving the likenesses and story of the native tribesmen among whom he was born and spent the major part of his life.

It has been made apparent there is an intimate affinity between music and art; and that one lends substance to the other. Be that as it may, Bob Scriver has accomplished the infinite in his bronze portrayals of the Blackfeet Indians.

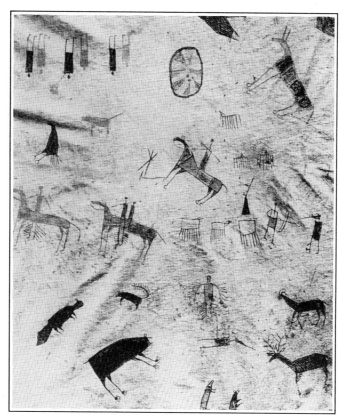

Painted Lodge Skin

This dressed skin of a buffalo cow was a portion of the lining of a lodge on which was painted pictures of important events in the life of Running Crane, a Blackfeet warrior. The skin measures about five by seven feet.

FOREWORD

Dr. John C. Ewers

Senior Ethnologist
Smithsonian Institution, Washington, D.C.

When I first met Dr. Ewers in the 1940s, he was founding curator of the Museum of the Plains Indian. It was immediately apparent to me that he was an outstanding person and a true scholar. His in-depth observations of the native people here and his accurate and carefully written anecdotes and notes resulted in several authoritative books about the Blackfeet.

He is universally recognized as the greatest living authority on these people, and it is to my deep satisfaction that he has written this foreword. I have made a sincere effort to make this work authentic and not in the least sensational in the "Hollywood" sense, and Dr. Ewers has aided me with extremely helpful comments and precise criticisms about some of the early pieces ("No More Buffalo" and "Return of the Blackfeet Raiders," in particular). He has played a significant part in the ultimate completion of this project.—R.M.S.

NO MORE BUFFALO

An Artist's Unique Tribute to the Blackfeet

No other North American Indians have held such a fascination for white artists as have the three Blackfoot tribes of Montana and Alberta. One hundred fifty years ago this summer, George Catlin, in the course of his extensive travels among more than fifty tribes who then lived beyond the frontier of white settlements, met a band of Blackfeet who were trading at the American Fur Company's newly established post of Fort Union at the mouth of the Yellowstone on the Upper Missouri. There he painted from life the earliest known series of portraits of these picturesque Indians.

Catlin considered his portrait of their chief, Buffalo Bull's Back Fat, an outstanding example of his Indian portraiture. While he was in Paris in 1846, he entered it in the world-famous Paris Salon. Not only was it accepted, along with one other of that artist's works, but it also won high praise from the famed French critic, Charles Beaudelaire, who wrote in admiration of Catlin's skill in capturing "the proud, free character, and noble expression" of his Indian subjects. Through the years that portrait of Buffalo Bull's Back Fat has been selected repeatedly for inclusion in exhibits of Indian portraits in this country and abroad, and it has been reproduced in color in numerous books on the art of the Old West. I recall that in 1963, after John F. Kennedy became president of the United States, the original of this oil portrait was borrowed from the collections of the Smithsonian Institution by the White House to hang on the wall behind that president's desk in the Oval Office.

Only a year after Catlin painted that portrait, the talented, young Swiss artist, Karl Bodmer, accompanied the able German naturalist, Maximilian, Prince of Wied-Neuwied, still farther up the Missouri, into the heart of the Blackfoot country. They spent a month at the trading post of Fort McKenzie observing the Blackfoot Indians nearby and recording their observations in notes and pictures. Like Catlin, young Bodmer made portraits of prominent tribal leaders. He also executed a panoramic view of their great circle camp of tipis and a vivid pictorial record of the action in a dawn attack upon a small camp of Piegan by a larger number of Cree and Assiniboin just outside the palisaded walls of Fort McKenzie on August 28, 1833, an event both the German naturalist and the artist witnessed from the elevated walkway just inside the palisade.

The publication and wide dissemination of Catlin's and Bodmer's portrayals of the Blackfeet encouraged many artists of later generations to visit and to picture those Indians from life. From the decade of the 1840s, a number of other artists traveled thousands of miles to observe and to draw or paint the Blackfoot Indians in their home territory. Some came from as far away as England and the European mainland, and their works have become almost as well-known abroad as they are in the United States and Canada. It is especially noteworthy that both Charles M. Russell and Frederic Remington spent some time sketching and learning about the Blackfeet firsthand not long before they began to gain national recognition as outstanding artist-interpreters of the Old West.

Among the many non-Indian artists who have sought to portray the appearance and customs of the Blackfeet, Bob Scriver may be considered to be unique—from several points of view. In the first place, he did not have to be lured to the Blackfoot country from afar—he was born there. Bob's father was the proprietor of a major early-twentieth-century trading post on the Blackfeet Reservation, the Browning Mercantile Company in the center of the little Agency town of Browning. Older Indians who spoke little or no English knew Bob's father by the name of Stumickahtose, meaning Medicine Bull. They came to know young Bob by a name which translated into English as Little Medicine Bull. Bob's schoolmates and playmates were grandchildren of those old Indians.

Members of the oldest generation of tribesmen in Bob's boyhood had themselves been born in buffalo-hide-covered tipis in the days when buffalo ran and when teenaged boys were impatient to join experienced warriors in raids upon enemy camps of Crow, Flathead, Cree or Assiniboin Indians. Bob retains vivid recollections of old Mountain Chief, son of a prominent Piegan war chief of the same name. In Bob's youth, Mountain Chief lived in a frame house near the

Agency in front of which a wooden sign informed the reader that Mountain Chief was the hereditary chief of the tribe. Every morning at sunrise, old Mountain Chief walked from his home to the Government Square, faced east and greeted the rising sun in his native tongue "in tones so clear and piercing that he could be heard by everyone in town." Probably Bob did not know that Mountain Chief, like many other men of his generation, was also an amateur artist. During the first decade of this century, he was one of the Indians who provided information on traditional Blackfoot social and religious customs to the anthropologist, Clark Wissler. A number of Mountain Chief's drawings of sacred objects (such as shields, headdresses, war shirts, and pipes) appear in Wissler's classic study *Ceremonial Bundles of the Blackfoot Indians*, published by the prestigious American Museum of Natural History of New York City seventy years ago.

Bob also tells me that he recalls that in his boyhood old Green-Grass-Bull and his wife furnished laundry water to the housewives of Browning. They filled water barrels from nearby Willow Creek and made their rounds with a horse-drawn wagon. In winter they used a bobsled. Not until many years later did Bob learn that this old water-carrier had been a warrior as a young man and had undergone the excruciating self-torture in the sun dance of his people.

Both of these old Indians were living when I arrived in Browning in the early spring of 1941 to become the first curator of the still-unfinished Museum of the Plains Indian just west of town, south of the site of the Indians' annual sun dance encampments and east of the fairgrounds where horse races and rodeos were held. Mountain Chief died later that year, but not before he had served as a valuable consultant to his grandnephew, Victor Pepion, in developing the details of his preliminary drawings for the series of colorful mural paintings Victor executed on the four walls of the museum lobby. The paintings interpreted the progress of a buffalo hunt as it might have occurred on that very site a century earlier.

I also came to know Green-Grass-Bull as one of my most knowledgeable informants on a variety of subjects ranging from warfare and religion to traditional crafts. Green-Grass-Bull was the dean of Blackfoot pipemakers at that time. Since his death, I have found some effigy pipes he had carved during his young manhood in the collection of a major eastern museum. Bob Scriver and I both remember that Green-Grass-Bull was a dog-lover who always seemed to have a large following of miscellaneous mongrels when he was seen walking the streets of Browning. In the collections of the Smithsonian Museum, I found a dog travois made by Green-Grass-Bull and collected some years before my time.

Unlike other non-Indian artists who have portrayed Blackfoot Indians, Bob Scriver's interest in doing this developed years after he first came to know them. It was only after his return to Browning as a mature man in 1951 that he turned his attention to sculpture—portraying first the many wild animals of the Glacier National Park and northwestern plains regions and later the Indians of the tribes he knew so well from his earliest days. As he began to create Indians in miniature, he recognized the need to immerse himself in the history and culture of these Indians if he were to portray them accurately in every detail. So Bob avidly read everything he could find on the Blackfeet in print. And as his knowledge increased so did his interest in all aspects of traditional tribal life—most especially in those traditional religious beliefs and rituals which survived long after their old-time staff of life, the buffalo, became extinct.

Bob Scriver's *No More Buffalo* is indeed unique. It is literally the product of a lifetime of seeking to understand the Blackfoot Indians. Through words and photographs of a truly remarkable series of sculptured works, Bob has sought to trace the history of an Indian people from prehistoric times before the pedestrian buffalo hunters acquired horses, through the years of contact with whites, to the extermination of the buffalo, and adaptation to reservation life. Through it all, these vital people have shown not only an ability to adapt to changed conditions but also a determination to retain those values they have held most dear. *No More Buffalo* is Bob Scriver's unique tribute to his lifelong friends, the Blackfeet.

BEFORE THE HORSE

Ceremonial Bundle for
the Lodge of Miscinskee (the Badger Tipi)

As this sculptural essay on the history of the Blackfeet unfolds, the figure of a solitary aborigine sitting on a rocky pinnacle creates the feeling of man preparing to rise to meet the challenges of his environment. Silhouetted by Sun, whose lifegiving energy has become the dominant Power in his life, he ponders what the future holds for him and The People. "Spoo-Moe-Kit, Nah-Too-Si" (Help me, Oh Sun) would also be an appropriate title for this sculpture.

These primitives were wild . . . as wild and free as any of the creatures that roamed the prairies with them. With the eyes of the eagle, the hearing of the deer, the cunning of the coyote and the endurance and stamina of the wolf, they lived in harmony with nature and survived. They were armed with only a stone-tipped spear and throwing stick (atlatl). In summer, these early Blackfeet went barefoot and naked among the rocks and prickly pear of the country and in winter would wrap themselves in the hides of animals they had killed.

According to linguists, the Blackfeet are of Algonkian stock. It is generally supposed among students of these matters that a small band of Algonkian-speaking people migrated westward above the Great Lakes region to live mainly on the northern border of the Saskatchewan plains. A brave and adventurous band of hunters, they pushed ever toward the West.

Upon reaching the Rockies, they gradually moved southward, forcing the Kootenai, Flathead, Snake and Crow out of the area. By the early 1800s, the Blackfeet controlled a huge territory reaching from the North Saskatchewan River in Canada south to the present Yellowstone Park area in Montana and east from the Continental Divide to about four hundred miles into what is now western North Dakota. This area included many thousands of miles of prime buffalo country.

The French and British traders got along well with the Blackfeet, but the unfortunate incident with Captain Lewis on the Marias River in 1806 (see page 68) turned the Blackfeet against the American trespassers. Thereafter, the warriors held at bay the encroachment of the Americans and all white settlement until after the Baker Massacre of 1870. The early British traders encouraged antagonism toward the Americans because they had been trading with the Blackfeet for several years and wanted to protect this brisk business. When Lewis and Clark came through the country, they discovered that the Blackfeet had guns and trade goods that had been obtained from the British.

The first Americans killed by the Blackfeet were probably fur trappers. Among them was John Potts who had been to the Pacific with the Lewis and Clark expedition. He had been given permission to leave the expedition to return to trap beaver in Blackfeet country and subsequently married a Blackfeet woman. He was slain in 1807 by a Blackfeet war party near the Three Forks area in southwest Montana. When the discovery of gold in 1862 brought an influx of prospectors, the Blackfeet sent many of them to the Great Beyond with the aid of a well-aimed arrow.

Isolated ranchers were likewise harassed by marauding war parties. In 1868, the killing of Malcolm Clark, a rancher living a short distance west of present-day Helena, Montana, finally sparked an all-out war between the races. General Phil Sheridan ordered Colonel E. M. Baker to muster his army unit at Fort Shaw and bring the offenders to justice. In Sheridan's words, "I want them struck . . . strike them hard!" In spite of a twenty degrees below zero temperature, Colonel Baker set out on a 150-mile forced march to arrest the murderers of Malcolm Clark, who were reported to be members of Mountain Chief's band. A camp was discovered on the Marias River, and at first light Baker's forces struck it unmercifully. It was not the camp of Mountain Chief but that of Heavy Runner's peaceful band! Thus, a terrible, swift and brutal retaliation was suffered by an innocent band of non-combatants. However, because of this action, the year 1870 saw the cessation of open hostilities of the Blackfeet toward the Americans.

The Blackfeet, having originated in Canada, became reservation Indians with the signing of Treaty Number 7 in Alberta on September 22, 1877. The Bloods, the North Piegan and the North Blackfoot still live north of the American boundary, but the South Piegan, now called Blackfeet, remain in northwestern Montana. The Montana Blackfeet first signed a treaty with the United States government in 1855, establishing their reservation agency at Fort Benton. The lucrative buffalo robe trade that was carried on with the Americans at Fort Benton on the Missouri was a turning point in the Indians' attitude toward the traders. Still, as noted previously in the account of Malcolm Clark's death, this period was not without incident. The agency was moved near Choteau in 1869, then to Badger Creek in 1876 and finally to Browning in 1895 where it remains the administrative headquarters for the Montana Blackfeet.

In 1780 there were an estimated fifteen thousand Blackfeet living from the North Saskatchewan River to the Yellowstone. This number was nearly halved by a terrible smallpox epidemic that swept through the camps in the late 1700s when Piegan warriors attacked a Shoshoni village that was infected with the disease. Not knowing about the transmission of infection, they unwittingly carried the disease back to their own camp in the contaminated loot taken from the Shoshonis. Today, however, they number approximately 18,000 if all the Blackfeet living in Canada and the United States are counted.

BEFORE THE HORSE

In the days before the horse, the family was a small unit consisting of a man, a woman and their offspring whose daily struggle was for mere survival. Clothed in poorly prepared animal skins, their possessions were few—mostly stone-tipped tools and weapons. Dogs were the principal beasts of burden, and anything that could not be loaded on them was placed on the backs of the woman and children. To be ready to ward off attacks from an enemy or a dangerous wild animal at a moment's notice, the man carried only his weapons.

The dogs—huge, ferocious animals, probably semi-domesticated wolves—were either loaded with a backpack or harnessed to a V-shaped framework of small poles, called a travois, onto which were placed the family's belongings. A leash on these dogs was necessary; otherwise, upon sighting game, they would give chase, scattering the family's meager possessions far and wide. It is said by the old

4

people that babies who were carried on these dog travois were sometimes lost in the long prairie grass when the dogs broke loose to chase game.

These were nomadic hunters who followed the migrations of the great herds of buffalo. They could travel only as far as they could walk in a day and were constantly on the alert for camping spots where they could find water and caves or overhanging rocks for shelter. At times a rude hut of brush was erected.

Weapons consisted of a club made of a rock tied with rawhide to a wooden handle, a short, flint-tipped jabbing spear and a long bow with several flint-tipped arrows. A flint skinning knife would complete the arsenal. Flint knives and arrow points were quite sharp—as sharp as any piece of broken glass. Many a buffalo was skinned with these "crude" flint knives, and many an enemy bit the dust with one of these arrow points in his back.

In the long ago, fire was created by the use of fire sticks, but as the culture advanced and people became many, a fire horn was used to carry the live coals from one camping spot to the next. This implement was a

buffalo horn lined with moist, rotted wood and fitted at the open end with a stopper. The carrier of the horn would select a live coal from the fire and place it with a piece of punk inside this almost airtight chamber. It was the carrier's responsibility to keep the coal alive. Later, fire steels were introduced by the traders which, when struck with flint, could produce the spark needed to start a fire.

In early days, a woman's hair was her only head covering, but a man sometimes used a cap of some animal's skin, usually with the ears left on as an aid in camouflage for hunting or as a good luck headpiece. The garments for a man and a woman were simply an animal skin suspended from one shoulder and tied by using the legs that were left on the hide. An undergarment for women was nonexistent, but for men a support much like the athletic supporter of today was used. Footwear consisted of tanned hides cut and sewn with a seam up the back and around the outside of the foot. In winter, skins were worn with the fur on the inside for warmth. Leggings were used as protection from thorn bushes and rattlesnakes.

Children generally went naked until puberty, and early explorers even recorded seeing children playing in the snow barefoot and naked. So the weak died early; only the strongest survived.

It is difficult to imagine that the Blackfeet lived—and even thrived—in this harsh climate where winter temperatures can dip to forty degrees below zero with winds of fifty miles an hour or more. These primitives, living in caves or brush shelters, were a hardy race. Centuries later, when they got the horse and lived in skin lodges, life became much easier.

The Way It Was

Each member of this primitive society contributed what he could for the benefit of all. With old age came the loss of teeth, dimness of vision, and feebleness of limb, so the old ones who had outlived their usefulness and had become a burden to the group were simply left by the trail for death to overtake them. Among the early Blackfeet, when it was decided that an old one must be left, she would be provided with enough food to last several days, and the camp would quietly slip away in the early light of dawn. When the old one awoke and saw them moving off in the distance, she would cry out over and over again, "NEETAH-KAH-YUCKI . . . Neetah-Kah-Yucki . . . neetah-kah-yucki." ("Never mind, you. Go—for I am many, I am many.") This meant, of course, that though she must die, she had left many offspring to carry on. That is the way it was in the long ago days before the coming of elk-dog.

This sculpture shows an old woman who has become a burden to the group and is left to die on the prairie. As she clutches her tattered robes about her, the symbolic bird-person of Death hovers over her, beckoning. Its one hand gently touches her shoulder, and the other firmly grasps her upreaching hand. She is prepared to die with dignity as she cries out, "NEETAH-KAH-YUCKI . . . Neetah-Kah-Yucki . . . neetah-kah-yucki. . . ."

7

Coming of Elk-Dog

Ho! What a surprise it must have been to these primitive Blackfeet when they first saw a horse. In this sculpture, the elders of the clan are explaining by hand signs what the strange animal is. With his arms raised and his first two fingers and thumb extended, one of the elders makes the sign for elk. Although the creature has no horns and lacks other elk-like features, it is the same size and color so he signs for elk and calls it "Ponokah" (Elk).

Another elder says he has seen it down south in an enemy camp dragging an "o-nes-stee" (travois) like a dog, and even though it is much larger and has hard feet (hooves), he signs for dog by placing the thumb and first two fingers of his right hand together, indicating its footprint, and calls it "Eemetah" (Dog).

Thus, the group decides that it is both Elk and Dog and so name this strange new beast "Ponokah-Eemetah" (Elk-Dog). This is still the word for horse among the Blackfeet.

This story is fictional, of course, because in all probability unmounted Blackfeet were attacked by mounted warriors from an enemy tribe to the south and hence got their first exposure to the horse. At first, the Blackfeet must have been panic-stricken, but as they studied the situation, it must have become apparent that they were at a serious disadvan-

tage and could even be wiped out unless they captured some of these strange animals. They soon obtained a few and learned how to use them. Their herds grew, and before long their entire mode of life was changed forever.

Previously, the Blackfeet had warred on a very small scale, and intertribal fighting had been generally carried out as a private grudge on a one-to-one basis. In dog days, raiding was of little practical value because people had few possessions that others would want, and even if they could capture the possessions of others, dog travois and the backs of people would seriously limit the amount of plunder to be carried away. After the horse was obtained and its many uses became apparent, a whole new way of life evolved which came to be known as the Horse Culture.

At about the same time that the Blackfeet got the horse (mid-1700s), they also acquired a few of the early trade muskets. These muskets really did not do much damage, but the effect of the great explosion when fired was devastating to the morale of an enemy, and so the mounted Blackfeet armed with his "thunder stick" grew very aggressive and quickly became the "Terror of the Northwestern Plains."

Acquisition of the horse helped make the Plains Indians into the freest people the world has ever known. They became mobile in war; their garments, their dwellings and their food were more easily obtained; their personal belongings and their religious bundles became much more expansive. In the opinion of many, mankind reached its zenith with the combination of the Plains Indian and the horse. Having little or no government, they lived the rich, free, unfettered life so many modern people yearn for.

THE HORSE

THE FIRST HORSE

The first horse that the Plains Indians encountered was probably the Spanish Barb or a direct descendant of that breed. In 1493, during Columbus' second trip to the New World, the rugged little Spanish Barbs were first put ashore on Santo Domingo Island in the Caribbean Sea and from there were taken to the mainland. The natives were terrified of these strange beasts at first but soon got to appreciate their worth. Some of these ponies escaped the conquistadores and the Caribbean Indians and ran free to breed and multiply. With the help of natural migration and the trading of horses among various tribes, the Blackfeet obtained them in the 1700s.

The Barb is a small horse (under fourteen hands high) with an average weight of about eight hundred pounds. Its back is shorter than other breeds in that it has only five lumbar vertebrae with seventeen pairs of ribs. This short back gives it the ability to turn on a dime. Barbs can run long distances and are as surefooted as a mountain goat. Their coat ranges from slate to dun and buckskin. Mane, tail and hooves are black, as are the legs from the knee down. Both mane and tail are long.

This little pony is not much of a horse by today's standards, but it had good wind and tough, durable hooves. It was able to travel great distances with little water and could subsist on a wide variety of forage. In winter, it would readily paw through snow to get at the grass, and when food was scarce, it could live off shrubs and the bark of aspen or cottonwood trees. When the ponds and rivers lay frozen, snow would serve as its water supply. Range stock of this area today are released in the fall to survive the winter as best they can. Because many western range horses have bloodlines tracing back to the Barb, they winter well unless deep snow comes to the range and the wind fails to blow it from the ridges.

During the Indian wars, these wiry little Indian ponies, without benefit of iron shoes, could outwalk, outrun and outdistance the large grain-fed, iron-shod cavalry horses. The big, handsome army horse was no match for this small, rugged mustang of the plains, for without grain and iron shoes the cavalry horse became practically immobile. U. S. generals who met the mounted plains warriors in battle called them the best light cavalry in the world. Indian ponies were trained to be mounted from either side, to lead and be hobble-wise and picket-wise. They could be neither gun-shy nor fearful of the sounds of battle. A pony was broken to ride by getting him into belly-deep water or into a large mudhole where the rider would have the most advantage.

Shown in this sculpture is a Barb horse that has been captured by three young warriors. The pony, having been picketed and neither fed nor watered for a few days in order to make him weaker and easier to manage, is being held by the ears and nose so that a bridle of some sort can be fitted to his head. When all is ready, one of the young men will leap on the horse's back, and with a kick and a yell the two will go bucking and running across the prairie. Eventually the horse will tire, and the man will be able to bring him under control, the start of a long and patient training program aimed at the making of a good buffalo-chasing horse. If the pony shows unusual talent, he might be made into a fine war horse. But, if after prolonged training the horse still shows no aptitude for buffalo-chasing or war, he will be given to the women as a camp-moving horse.

A Warrior's Prize

The pursuit of war was the all-consuming passion of the Blackfeet warrior; groups of young men were constantly on the move, either coming back from or going out on the war trail. Much of the conversation of the old men in camp concerned their exploits against the enemy. Each took his turn recounting his coups (a French word pronounced *kooz*, meaning "blows") and reliving youthful memories of the war trail.

Foremost among the great deeds of valor was stealing the favorite war pony from the lodge of an enemy chief. Taking a large number of horses or an ordinary pony was a worthy coup, but in no way could it compare with the taking of a famous war horse or buffalo-runner. Great war horses and exceptional buffalo-runners were as well-known by warriors of opposing tribes as our own great race horses, such as Man-of-War and Secretariat, are known to us. It was these ponies that were wonderful prizes for the young men who could take them. When enemy tribes occasionally made peace, there was always much talk about these special horses.

At night, such horses were always tied close by their owner's lodge with the picket rope attached to the sleeping owner's wrist. With the horse guarded in this manner, as well as by the owner's dogs, it was no mean feat to creep into the enemy camp after dark, cut the tether and tough rawhide hobbles and remove the animal from the midst of the camp. Stealers of horses were uncanny in their ability to do just that. The challenge was extremely exhilarating, and success would gain all the glory a young man could hope for. On the other hand, failure could mean certain death or torture at the hands of the enemy.

The horse was so important to these people that to own one became an obsession. Important warriors counted their wealth in the hundreds of horses they owned. Playing children would scamper around with their chins tucked against their chests imitating a galloping horse with neck bowed; or tucking their arms against their breasts like a rearing horse, they would utter a shrill whinny as they pretended to be warriors riding into battle or stallions fighting. Amulets, horse war medicines, effigies, stylized drawings on robes, tipi linings and lodge skins were some of the ways in which respect for the horse was shown in the Blackfeet culture.

GRANDFATHER TELLS OF THE HORSE

A great warrior once had a dream about a place where many horses were to be had just for the taking. He announced that he was going to this place to make a surprise raid, and many young warriors wanted to join this man because his medicine was good and his luck strong.

The old man at the left in the sculpture, now a grandfather, was among those young men who went. The women from his father's lodge prepared pemmican and made extra moccasins. The male relations outfitted him with everything he needed for war—rope, whip, knife, arrows and bow. He prepared his own war amulet and headdress.

The leader of the raid set the approximate time and day of departure, but to keep the party as small as possible, the exact time was kept secret to all but a chosen few.

Once on the trail, the group stopped and together held a sweat bath to purify themselves and sang their wolf (war) songs. They smoked the pipe for good luck and prayed to Sun, Earth and the Four Directions. After the sweat bath, they all ran to the river and plunged in.

At the start, the group traveled in daylight, but as danger of discovery by the enemy became greater, they traveled by night. In the group were both seasoned warriors and several young men learning the ways of the war trail, who were allowed on this raiding party as servants for the more experienced warriors. The young men carried the extra moccasins, the extra pemmican, ropes, blankets and weapons. They also gathered firewood and packed water. The leading warriors, performing none of these menial tasks, concentrated on the strategy for the entire war party.

As the raiding party approached enemy country, scouts were sent out. Keeping well hidden in coulees and behind rocky outcroppings, they would signal whether the enemy was in sight. When the enemy was located, the men would paint themselves, each in his own manner according to his dream vision, and war amulets and other good luck items were put on.

Then after dark they would cautiously approach the enemy camp carrying only a knife and rope. The leader would pick several proven warriors known for their calm nerve and sound judgment to go with him into the enemy camp to cut the ropes of the prized horses. The others of the party remained outside the camp to hold the horses as the "catchers" brought them out.

This grandfather remembers how, at a certain time, the leader motioned for him to go into the enemy camp to try his luck. Before darkness came, he had noticed a fine black and white horse on the far side of the camp. He knew that he might have only this one chance to prove his ability as a taker of horses. He crept to the far side of the camp, cut the beautiful stallion loose and went on out the same side, circling back around to where the rest were waiting. Driving and leading the horses stealthily away until they were out of earshot of the camp, the warriors each mounted a horse and rode off driving the stolen herd before them. With a light-sleeping enemy and many camp dogs to contend with, the taking of enemy horses was a thrilling experience.

So, as this Blackfeet grandfather spins his tale to his grandsons, they learn how he crept into the camp of the enemy and took the prize stallion of the war chief; of how he rode the great horse on many exciting chases after Ee-Nee, the buffalo; and of how, mounted on the same mighty war horse, he charged the enemy and with the speed of the wind escaped all his pursuers after counting coup on one of them. The grandsons are held enraptured and vow that they will be mighty warriors like Grandfather—they too will steal many horses from the enemy and will ride their black and white stallions on many successful raids.

HUNTING

In the days before the horse, buffalo were sometimes taken by driving them over cliffs. Two rows of piled boulders formed in a huge V extended a mile or more along each side of the proposed jump-off site. To direct the fleeing buffalo, people would wait in hiding behind these piles of rocks.

A piskun (corral) was built of logs and tightly woven brush at the bottom of the cliff to hold those animals not killed in the fall. Buffalo would not try to go through this seemingly solid wall; but if they saw a glimmer of light, they would attempt to escape. Women, children and some hunter-marksmen hid behind this barricade, and arrow after arrow was shot into the animals as they milled around in the enclosure. Because of the Blackfeet superstition against using an arrow a second time, these buffalo drive sites are rich in flint points of all sizes. These drives were an efficient way to get meat for all the people.

Before the drive, a holy man unwrapped his Pipe and prayed to Sun and to all his Powerful Helpers for a successful drive. The young man chosen to be the decoy participated in a sweat bath for purification and prayed that the buffalo might follow him and that he might not stumble into a badger hole or be run down by the onrushing animals. He would tell his women relations to stay in the lodge and to burn the Holy Sweet Grass while praying for his success.

When all was ready, he arose before daylight and, donning his buffalo decoy robe, went out on the prairie to where the animals were bedded down. The people took their assigned stations behind the piles of rocks. The young man's task of luring the herd into the V of rocks and on over the cliffs was all-important. He had to know the habits of the buffalo as if he were one himself so, having smeared himself with the dung of buffalo to hide his man-scent, the decoy closely approached the herd and by devious acts tried to entice a buffalo to follow him. Soon, an inquisitive cow or young bull would take one step toward him, then another and another. By his actions, the decoy would attract the attention of several of the other animals, then he would continue to work patiently until the herd began a general movement in his direction, first at a walk, then faster and faster and on into the V of rocks where the people were hiding.

When the herd had passed their particular vantage points, the people would rise up shouting and waving robes to frighten the herd onward to its fatal plunge. It was impossible for the front-running buffalo to slow their pace or change direction once the herd was in full flight. Still, these drives were not always successful because at times the lead animals would suddenly veer off to one side or the other away from the trap. If the herd escaped and became scattered over the prairie, the buffalo could scarcely ever be enticed into the V again; hence every precaution was taken to prevent this from happening. The young decoy had to be very fleet of foot. At the crucial moment, he had to throw aside his robe and race to dodge behind one of the rock piles to escape being trampled to death by the onrushing animals, as shown in this sculpture.

There are many places in Blackfeet country where these drives have taken place (see page 128). Layers of bones at the base of these cliffs provide evidence of long, continuous use of certain corral sites. One such piskun, excavated by a team of scientists sponsored by the Hill Family Foundation under the direction of Dr. Tom Kehoe, is about six miles northeast of Browning. Alternating layers of bones and charcoal indicate that the unused carcasses and the corrals were burned after each drive. This area is rich in archeological material, especially spear and arrow points. From time to time, I was called upon to identify various bone fragments; among these were elk, deer, antelope, coyote and fox, which showed that animals other than bison were caught in the drives.

THE BUFFALO HORSE

Once the buffalo were located, each hunter hurriedly caught his favorite mount—a spirited, long-winded runner. To conserve the energy of his hunting horse, he rode an ordinary one and led the other. Keeping to the coulees, the hunters moved as close as they could to the herd, being ever mindful to keep out of sight. Constant attention was given to the wind direction, since the herd would run off if the man-scent was detected. At a signal from the hunt chief, the men dismounted and prepared their hunting horses. When all were ready, the chief gave the signal, and the chase was on. Each hunter killed as many buffalo as he could—young dry cows for meat and lodge covers, bulls for shields and heavy rawhide items. In the days before the gun, owner-marked arrows could identify the kill, but with gun-killed animals, arguments as to whose buffalo it was sometimes occurred.

Riding equipment was kept to a minimum. A rope surcingle was tied tightly around the horse just in back of its front legs. The rider would place his knee and heel under this rope in such a manner that should his horse fall he would be able to extricate himself easily. A simple war bridle was used as part of the guiding system, although a well-trained buffalo pony responded to knee pressure and the body movement of the rider much like a well-trained calf-roping horse of today. Attached to the reins was a long thong of hide tied to make a slip noose around the neck of the horse. This thong trailed so that if the rider were unhorsed, he would have a chance to catch the trailing thong, thereby causing the slipknot to choke the horse and slow it down so that he could mount again.

The preferred weapon was a strong short bow and a quiver full of arrows. Some hunters used a short jabbing spear in addition to the bow and arrow, while others used the one shot muzzle-loading trade gun. The number of buffalo killed by these food-gathering Indians with their primitive weapons scarcely made a dent in the population of the massive herds.

The slaughter began in earnest with the hunters' introduction to the Winchester repeating rifles (the Henry in 1860, the Yellow Boy in 1866, the famous Winchester Model 1873) and the deadly 50-calibre Sharps wielded by white hide-hunters. In the 1870s, the buffalo were counted in the millions, yet by 1883 they were practically extinct. A great many were killed for the tongue only, a delicacy in the east; the carcass was left to rot on the prairie. During World War I, trainload after trainload of buffalo bones were shipped east to be processed into nitrates for gunpowder and fertilizer. Even now, one can sometimes find a skull, a leg, or other bone fragments buried in unbroken prairie sod—the last remains of the massive herds that at one time stretched from horizon to horizon.

One of the greatest thrills imaginable is to ride a good horse on a wild chase after buffalo. I have a little grey half-Arabian pony, Gunnysack, that qualifies as a real buffalo-runner. I rode him in five of the annual bison roundups at the Moiese National Bison Range. He would dance with excitement at the sight of buffalo, and when the command came to run them, he was off like the wind. On several occasions, I rode up alongside a chosen buffalo and pretended to shoot an arrow into the lung cavity which is back of the rib cage. My pony would easily get me into the right position.

A buffalo can run farther than a horse at continued high speed, but a good horse can catch and even pass a buffalo in a short run. Cow buffalo can run faster than the bulls and are also the best meat. In winter, when the fur becomes silky and thick, their hides make the finest robes. Young bulls are quite fast and are the next best choice for meat. Old bulls are seldom taken, as the meat is tough and they are the most dangerous and hardest to kill. Many a buffalo pony bears the scars of a close encounter with an enraged bull. A story is told at the National Bison Range of one of the riders and his horse being carried a hundred yards or more on the horns of a bull before becoming dislodged. The horse was disemboweled, and the rider seriously injured. Similar incidents must have happened when the Blackfeet hunters were running buffalo.

I had some narrow escapes on the roundups, but my little grey was very fast and extremely surefooted. When I got into trouble, I would just give him the rein and hang on. Gunnysack always got us both to safety. Once a huge bull charged so close to my horse's rump that I could have reached his head with a bow.

Bob Scriver on Gunnysack

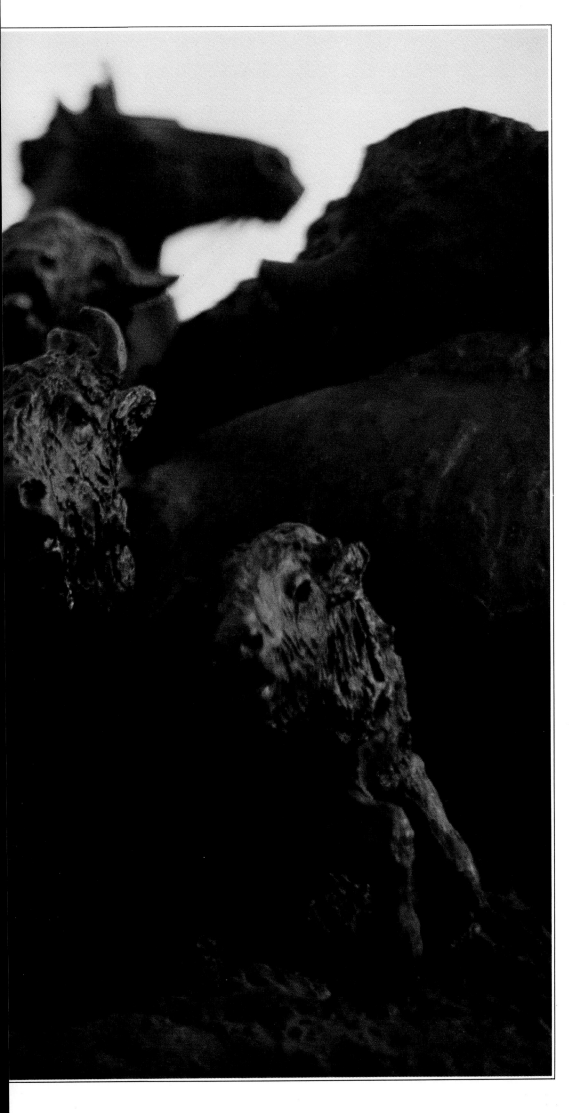

REAL MEAT

The Blackfeet word for buffalo is Ee-Nee which when translated relates to the black horns of the buffalo. Ee-Nee is a word in Blackfeet that is so ancient that its exact meaning has been lost. Buffalo meat was called "The Meat" or "The Real Meat" as compared to the other animals that were used for food, such as elk, deer, antelope and mountain sheep. Anything that was the best or most important was called "Real" or simply "The." The grizzly was "The Real Bear." Their own people were "The Real People" or "The People." Hence, I titled this sculpture of the hunting of buffalo "Real Meat."

Charles Russell did an outstanding bronze, "Wild Meat For Wild Men," on this theme. I wanted to sculpt this situation also but did not want it to be in the least a derivative of the Russell piece. Upon analyzing the basic composition of his sculpture, I found it to be based on a counter-clockwise movement ⟳ so I based my piece on an explosive design— ⇉ . Thus, though the subject matter is the same, the basic designs are entirely different.

Running buffalo at breakneck speed over the rough prairie was extremely dangerous. Not only could the beasts maim and kill both horse and rider, but badger holes and hidden washouts also presented additional dangers. If the animals

could be induced to mill around, a great many would be dispatched with arrow, lance or gun. But if a straightaway run occurred, the horses would soon become winded, and many of the buffalo would escape.

In this sculpture, the animals have just broken away and are beginning to escape. One hunter is in a dangerous position in their midst. He has thrust his lance deep into the rib cage of a young bull. This wound in the lung area means that the animal will be able to run only a short distance before he must stop. The hunters will return later to kill him. The other hunter is racing alongside a nice, fat cow buffalo, preparing to shoot an arrow into a vital spot.

This group of bison was modeled from actual animals thinned from the herd at the annual Fall Roundup at the National Bison Range, Moiese, Montana. The animals were all carefully measured with the most generous help of Range Superintendent C. J. Henry and Range Foreman Victor May. The big bull

stampeding buffalo. Then I discovered a broken chin strap on his bridle—which is like going down a highway at sixty miles an hour trying to stop and finding you have no brakes! I was indeed lucky that my pony was fast and surefooted.

YELLOW WOLF, SETTER OF SNARES

It is known that the Indian was an exceptionally successful trapper of animals for the early fur trade. Yet, Indians rarely used the steel trap as did their white counterparts. They preferred to fashion their traps on the spot from materials that were always close at hand. The Blackfeet had several ways of catching the fur-bearers whose pelts they could exchange for many wondrous and useful things from the Napikwan (white man) trader: the pit, the deadfall, the snare, the hang noose, the set bow, the bow and arrow (hand held), the rifle and the shotgun. Poison was seldom if ever used by the early Blackfeet.

The pit was a deep hole dug in a game trail, covered over and skillfully disguised. Deer, elk, bear and some of the smaller animals could be taken this way. Overall, this method was not often used.

The deadfall method used a heavy log balanced on a baited trip so that when the animal moved the trip, the log would crash down, either pinning the victim or killing it outright. This method was a favorite in heavily forested country, especially for furbearers such as lynx, bobcat and timber wolves.

The snare was made of stout gut, pliable leather or sinew. When wire was available, it was used on some sets where the snare was placed underwater for otter, beaver and muskrat. Snares were good for marten, fisher, mink, weasel and rabbit. Coyotes, lynx and bobcats could also be taken with snares.

The hang noose was a variation of the snare in which the animal disengaged a trip, and the snare, fastened to a bent-over sapling, jerked the victim high into the air. Snares of both types were extensively used.

Beaver, buffalo and wolf were the three furbearing animals that were sought most by white traders who were located at various posts throughout Indian country. Beaver were found in abundance all along the streams in the area of the Blackfeet, but they were not taken in as great numbers by the Indian hunters as by the white mountain men with their steel traps. Wolves also were not hunted as much by the Indians as by their white counterparts. The white wolfers trapped and poisoned this prey in large numbers.

on the left side of the sculpture actually measured twelve feet from tip to tip when stretched out the way he is shown.

The scene depicted by the sculpture is one that I have experienced. When we were running buffalo on one occasion, I suddenly found myself in the midst of a small herd unable to control my horse. I quirted Gunnysack harshly, and we burst right on through the herd. Finally, I managed to quiet him down enough to be able to dismount at a safe distance from the

However, buffalo were hunted extensively by the Blackfeet. The robes and hides from these animals were what the early Blackfeet traded for the white man's goods—blankets, beads, powder and ball, guns, knives, hatchets. The records of the early fur trade at Fort Benton, Montana, showed that tens of thousands of raw and tanned buffalo hides obtained from the Blackfeet were shipped on boats down the Missouri River to markets in the east.

The days of the wild buffalo and wolf are gone forever, but beaver and other small furbearers are taken by a few Blackfeet trappers even today.

I personally know a Blackfeet trapper who catches elk, deer, wolf, lynx and the smaller furbearers with a snare alone. His is a rare breed today but in the olden days was commonplace. His name is Yellow Wolf, a real old-time "setter of snares." Every winter he sets his snares as he has always done and lives the life of the solitary trapper in the wilds of the Rocky Mountain foothills in Blackfeet country.

CAMP
LIFE

The Hide Scraper

While the Blackfeet man was the hunter, protector and provider, the woman prepared the food, cared for the young, kept the lodge in order and made the clothing. The tanning of hides into warm, soft, pliable leather was hard, back-breaking labor. Deer hide was the favorite material for clothing while elk and buffalo were used for robes and footwear.

To prepare a raw hide for tanning, it is soaked in water for several days until the hair comes off easily when rubbed with a blunt stick or the palm of the hand. The hide is rather smelly at this point because in order for the hair and epidermis to loosen, a stage of slight decomposition must set in. The hide is next pegged down around the edges on a level piece of ground and allowed to dry. When the hide becomes quite hard, a scraper made from a sharpened chisel-like steel or a piece of flint attached to an elk horn is used to thin the hide to the desired thickness, as illustrated in this sculpture.

To tan the hide to pliable softness, it must be soaked again and then a solution of brains and other ingredients is applied. Next, the hide is rolled up to allow this solution to penetrate completely. After a day or so it is unrolled and allowed to dry a second time. At this point, it is stretched and pounded until all the fibers are broken down and there are no hard spots left. This will make white buckskin. Although white buckskin is very beautiful, it is not good

for everyday use because it will revert to rawhide if it gets wet. A tanned skin that has been smoked over a punky-smoky cottonwood fire, with color ranging from golden to a rich dark brown, remains pliable even if it gets wet. Some find its strong, pungent odor objectionable, but to those of us who have been raised wearing the Indian-tanned smoked buckskin, the aroma is delightful and brings back memories of pleasant times enjoying good company around a camp fire.

FIREWOOD

The constant chore of gathering wood for the lodge fires for warmth and cooking fell to the women. In the absence of saws and good axes, it was necessary to make camp where there was an abundance of easily gathered twigs and branches. Quaking aspen and cottonwood were favored because they burned warm with little ash and no sparks. Willow twigs were also used because they too made a warm and smokeless fire; willow, however, burned out rather quickly. Fir, pine and juniper were seldom used except where there was no other fuel available because although they burned well, they threw sparks which could be hazardous in a lodge having an open fire pit.

When camp was made on the prairie, dried patties of buffalo dung were used. These "buffalo chips" burned much like coal with an even, blue, smokeless flame and were probably the most widely used fuel by both Indians and whites in the early days out on the treeless prairies. The little valley where the Snake Creek flows in the Bear Paw Mountains and where Chief Joseph's hard-pressed band of Nez Percé survivors fought their last battle was known by all Indians as the "Place of the Many Manure Fires." It seems as though this was a favorite gathering spot for large numbers of buffalo; the ground was literally covered with dried buffalo patties.

Bob Scriver with Chief Earl Old Person at renaming of Running Eagle Falls

BLACKFEET FAMILY PORTRAIT

Most of these portraits are not of actual people but are composites of Blackfeet types. As we view the photograph starting from the lower righthand corner, we see the portrait of the young woman called Pitamahkan (Running Eagle), the most famous of Blackfeet women. James Willard Schultz has written a book based upon her exploits called *Running Eagle, the Warrior Girl.* When she was growing up, she was not one to play with dolls but preferred playing at war with her brothers. When she matured, a dream told her to go searching for a vision. In her quest, she went toward the place of the Two Medicine Lodges lakes and finally found sanctuary in a cavern under a mountain falls

that lies between the two lower lakes. There she fasted and in her vision saw that she should become a warrior.

The falls where she had her vision was ever after called Pitamahkan Falls (Running Eagle Falls) by The People. It lies within the boundaries of what is now Glacier National Park where park officials called it "Trick Falls" because water comes over the top and through a great hole halfway down (the vision place of Running Eagle). The falls is indeed "tricky," but this was hardly a dignified name for so beautiful a natural phenomenon steeped in the legends and history of the Blackfeet. In 1981, through the efforts of many inter-

ested people, park officials were persuaded to have this beautiful falls renamed "Running Eagle Falls."

During her lifetime Pitamahkan's exploits were many and her war parties were very successful. She was given the name Pitamahkan at one of the annual Sun Lodge ceremonies. In a rare honor for a woman, she was allowed to become a member of the all-male Brave Dogs' warrior society. After many adventures on the war trail, she was killed in a battle with the Flatheads.

The portrait of the young boy is the only one for which someone actually posed. Timmy, the son of my friends Carl and Carmelita Cree Medicine, posed for me when he was about four years of age. He liked to pose and said he would "work for me anytime."

The warrior figure is named White Quiver. White Quiver was a noted warrior and famous as a stealer of horses; his is an honored name among the Blackfeet. A favorite story is still told of the time he journeyed to the country of the Crows, took a bunch of horses and drove them alone across the international border into Canada (some 400 miles). He was caught by the Northwest Mounted Police, and he and the horses were impounded. At night, while the Mounties were asleep, he escaped, took the horses out of the compound, crossed the border back into the United States and returned to his reservation where he could not be taken. He did this deed alone—a coup still recounted by his relatives. An interesting anecdote is that this noted warrior lived here when I was a boy—in fact, he died, or "went to the Sand Hills," in 1932—the year I graduated from Browning High School.

The grandmother figure is so typically Blackfeet that people here on the reservation think they recognize her, but she is no one in particular. I call her Kip-Ah-Talk-Ee (Old Woman), a term of endearment.

The grandfather figure is a fine example of an older member whose hair is wrapped in the manner of a Thunder Medicine Pipe man. He is called Napi (Old Man) which is a term of respect in this usage—not to be confused with the Napi of legends. Elders among The People demand and receive a great deal of respect.

THREE COURTSHIP SCENES

The photograph on page 34 is a composite shot of three separate sculptures that share a common theme: courtship among the Blackfeet. A description of each of the separately titled pieces is give below.

PRAIRIE ROMANCE
(background)

Young girls learned to tan robes, prepare dry meat, make moccasins and perform all the many household tasks that would make her a desirable wife. The young men spent most of their time combing and braiding their hair and painting themselves in an attractive manner. Parading around the camp near the young women, each hoped that one would glance his way and that she would admire him.

AT THE SPRING
(middle)

When a young woman became of marriageable age, she was watched very closely by her parents and was seldom left alone. When she went to gather wood or fetch water from the spring, she was nearly always accompanied by an adult. The young men, on the other hand, were completely unhampered and uninhibited. And so, as has always been the case among the young, ways were found for a rendezvous. Young girls were shy but not unaware of a handsome young warrior's attention. As shown in this small sculpture, a favorite trysting place was at the spring where the maiden went to fetch water.

THE PROPOSAL
(foreground)

Marriageable age for girls was reached at about fourteen summers, but at times they were promised at birth and actually married as early as the age of eight. When so young, the parents of the girl would select a husband for her. If she was mature and made the advances herself, she would carry food to her future husband's lodge and perhaps make him moccasins. If he accepted the gifts, she would move into his lodge. Of course, upon this mutual acceptance there was always a feast and the giving of presents.

If the parents of the man initiated the proposal, they would leave horses, gifts and other valuables at the door of the father-in-law-to-be. If the gifts were taken within, it meant that the young man was the successful suitor. If they were not taken in, it meant that he was rejected.

Marriage was taken seriously by the Blackfeet, and the taboo against unions between close kin undoubtedly accounted for their high mental and physical development. Since the work load for the wife of a successful hunter was extremely heavy, plural marriages were not only quite acceptable but also necessary. The man often married sisters, as he believed that they would be more apt to get along well together. The first wife, however, was as a rule the matriarch of the lodge and was known as the man's "sits-beside-him-woman."

Regarding moral standards, infidelity by the women was punished by facial mutilation, death or banishment. The husband or close male relatives passed the judgment. When I was a boy living on the reservation at Browning, I knew of two women who had their noses cut off. We kids called them "Old Nosies" in childhood derision. As I grew up and came to know more about these things, I learned that at one time they had been unfaithful to their husbands. Among The People they are known as "cut nose women."

Owner of the Lodge

The owner of the lodge was most certainly the master in his own home. His position was at the rear of the lodge where he rested on a bed of softly tanned buffalo robes facing the door. Inverted V-shaped backrests made from horizontally strung willow wands were suspended on decorated tripods made from sturdy lodgepole pine saplings. One was placed at each end of the bed.

Broadly speaking, lodge etiquette is quite strict. There are additional rules when the owner is the possessor of a dream-painted lodge that only the people acquainted with them will know. Medicine Bundle owners are subject to traditional restrictions, and every owner of a personal bundle has his own individual taboos.

Some general rules of etiquette in a Blackfeet lodge follow: one does not enter unless invited to do so; men visitors sit on the right as they enter with women on the left; a person never goes between the owner of the lodge and the center fire or altar, if there is one; the owner is never spoken to by a visitor unless he is invited to do so; a visitor does not sit down unless invited to do so, and then he is told where to sit; finally, the nearer he is seated to the owner, the more respect he is shown.

The smoking pipe is passed from right to left, starting with the owner of the lodge. It must never go past the doorway and so must be returned from left to right. Generally, before a social smoke, puffs are taken and blown to Sun, Earth and the Four Directions. The social smoke is taken as long as the person desires—usually ten to fifteen puffs.

Smoking material consists of kinnikinnick (bearberry leaves) mixed with tobacco. The aroma is very pleasant, but the smoke has a tendency to bite the tongue with its sharpness; hence the long-stemmed

pipe with a stone bowl is used most often. The stone bowl is made of a soft rock dug from river banks and carved into traditional shapes before it is baked and

hardened in the fire. Traditional Blackfeet pipe bowls are carved in a rather blunt, blocky style and are traditionally colored black. Sioux-style pipe bowls, by contrast, are generally long and slender and reddish in color. The location of the raw pipestone is a closely

guarded secret, and the "mining" of the stone is accompanied by prayers and gifts to the spirits.

The lodge of the plains people was a highly mobile unit and could be taken down or erected in a very short time. With a lining that extended about four feet up from ground level, it was warm in winter and cool in summer. Door openings always faced the east. Smoke

flaps at the apex were used to regulate ventilation and could be closed in bad weather.

Early day lodges were made of tanned skins of the buffalo. But as trade with the whites progressed and the buffalo became fewer, more and more lodge covers were made from white canvas. Nevertheless, a lodge cover is still called "lodge skin." Examples of the original skin covers are now found only in museums. The last skin lodge known to be in actual use by the Blackfeet was in 1896, a dream-painted lodge decorated with the crow (or raven) design.

A Blackfeet lodge is erected on a basic form of four poles. Nineteen poles plus two flap poles are required for the average lodge. Pegs to hold down the skin are placed through the loops provided at about one-and-one-half foot intervals along the bottom. A skillfully set up lodge is a very comfortable home, completely liveable in all seasons, and one of the great contributions that the Plains Indian has made to modern civilization. There is much more that can be said about Blackfeet lodges, the dream-painted lodges and lodge etiquette, but that would make a small volume in itself.

RECREATION

Gambling seems to be an innate part of human nature, and the Blackfeet are certainly among the foremost proponents of this ancient pastime. The Hand Game (or Stick Game) has become so much a part of their lives today that tournaments are held with prizes running into hundreds of dollars. In earlier days, losers were known to have gambled away all their worldly possessions.

The object of the game is to hide a set of bones from the opposing side much like "Button-button, which hand holds the button." The bones used in playing this game are four pieces of elk or deer antler about three and one-half inches in length and one inch in diameter. Two are plain and are called the long bones, two are decorated with a black band painted around the center and are called short bones. Players try to guess in which hand their opponents hold the long or unpainted bones.

Two rows of players numbering from eight to a dozen or more sit cross-legged on the ground facing each other. A log lying in front of each row is used as a drumming board. To keep score, eleven counting sticks (willow wands about twelve inches long and one-half inch in diameter) are stuck in the ground between the opposing sides. Five are painted yellow and five are painted red. The eleventh stick, called the kick stick, is painted half yellow and half red. By enacting a short preliminary "hiding the bones" game, it is used to determine which side will be first to hold the bones.

The game can be played with one or more bones-hiders, but two hiders is the usual number. During the changing of the bones from hand to hand, a spirited song is repeated over and over, accompanied by rapid drumming on the log. At a signal, an opponent points to the ones hiding the bones. If the correct hand is chosen, the opponent takes possession of the bones; but if the incorrect hand is chosen, the holder of the bones keeps the bones and takes possession of a counting stick. When one side wins all eleven sticks, it is declared winner, bets are paid and a new game is started.

It is difficult to say when all the games are over. I can only surmise that they end when the players are utterly exhausted or are completely out of money or trading stock.

The singing and tap-tap-tapping on the log drum lasts all four days of the Blackfeet Indian Days celebration held in mid-July and ceases only when camp is broken and everyone moves on to another song and dance fest.

WAITING FOR THE DANCE

During the general gathering of all The People for the annual Sun Dance celebration, there are many religious ceremonies and dances. Men and women both take part in these serious, mostly secret, affairs.

At the ceremony for the Medicine Pipe, each holy man in turn dances energetically with the Pipe or other

items in the bundle, while at the same time his woman dances by standing in place and raising up and down on the balls of her feet, keeping time with the music.

At certain points during the Beaver Bundle ceremony, the women dance with the beaver symbols while the men look on or merely sway in time with the music of the rattle. If the men dance, they do so alone.

There are public dances in addition to these ceremonial dances. The Round Dance of today evolved from the ancient Scalp-Lock Dance in which the women took a large part, dancing wildly about and showing off scalps that their successful warrior-husbands had taken from the enemy. With the passage of time, this became a dance in which men, women and children participated. It was a slow dance; all joined hands and moved sideways in a great circle giving the Round Dance its name. The accompanying drumbeat was a steady two-beat rhythm.

The other public dance is known as the Owl Dance. The drumbeat is a rather lively two-beat, hard-soft rhythm. Men and women generally dance together in pairs, and all pairs move in a clockwise direction. The dance step is a simple sideways shuffle and is very popular among young and old alike. Shown here is a shy young maiden waiting to be asked to dance by the young warrior of her heart.

DANCE CONTEST

An all-time favorite pastime with the Blackfeet is the dance. There are religious dances, war dances, scalp dances and victory dances, among others. These are serious, business-like functions, but there comes a time when social dancing just for the fun of it takes over, and everyone is free to participate.

The best singers, numbering from four to six, gather around a large drum. The drum is made from a wooden hoop covered with elk or deer rawhide that is put on wet and allowed to tighten. When sounded, such a drum may be heard for a mile or more on a quiet summer eve. Night after night at the annual Summer Encampment I have gone to sleep with the hypnotic throb of the drum in my ears and into my very being. The beat is either steady or a series of hard-soft strokes about the tempo of the human pulse, speeding up or slowing down as the mood of the particular dance demands. Social dancing is mainly done for the pure enjoyment of it, but inevitably, as with all people, the competitive spirit takes over, and contests are organized to determine who can dance the fanciest and liveliest.

The early-day dances were always done to pantomime an event or the activities of a certain bird or animal. For example, the Prairie Chicken Dance was a symbolic reenactment of the mating ritual of the prairie chicken. This dance is still performed, but it seems as though individual interpretations have taken over and much of the early symbolism has been lost. Nowadays it is simply called the "Fancy Dance" or "Grass Dance."

With the passing of intertribal wars and the mixing of the various Indian groups, a cross-culture in the dance has developed, and the dances of one tribe look very much like the dances of another. This is apparent in the social dances in which early symbolism seems to be unimportant. The meaningful religious Medicine Pipe Dance and other Holy Dances are still performed in the traditional manner.

In this sculpture I have shown dancers and drummers of the early 1900 Reservation Period before the performers started wearing the extremely elaborate costumes of today. These young men are dressed in traditional fancy or grass dance costumes. They have donned the feather dance bustle of various styles, trade bells, deer hair head pieces, and other items to hold and dance with. One dancer is doing his solo while his competitors look on awaiting their turn.

Little Brother Goes Swimming

Blackfeet children were completely uninhibited and allowed to do about whatever they wanted. However, although they were never physically chastised, they were taught how to act by example and at times by rather severe verbal ridicule. Little boys were taught about waging war, tracking, hunting game, and being brave and aggressive. For the young warrior-to-be, it was pointed out that it was much better to die when you were in the prime of life fighting a brave enemy warrior in glorious battle than to linger on into old age when no one wanted you and you became a burden to your family.

Young girls were taught not to be frivolous and silly but the sort of person who would accept responsibility and keep a good, orderly and clean lodge for her man. She was taught how to make fine moccasins, to tan soft robes and buckskin and to care properly for any sacred bundles her man might acquire.

In winter, the girls played at lodge-keeping and the boys with spinning tops on smooth ice. The boys also played with buffalo rib sleds and hunted small game with their bows and arrows. Then when summer came and the ice left the ponds and rivers, all the children, both boys and girls, spent hour after hour swimming and playing in the water. All the kids would crowd onto the old family horse and head for the swimming hole. This sculpture depicts a common scene during the warm summer days at a Blackfeet camp.

THE HORSE RACE

Blackfeet were extremely proud of their horses. After the horse was introduced to them in the mid 1700s, a new culture was developed that was centered around the horse and its use. Every Blackfeet camp had large herds. Mares with colts, stallions and geldings, camp nags and fine runners were all intermingled. Pinto was a favorite color with blacks and bays being close seconds.

Even today the Blackfeet are very horse-oriented; some ranchers have herds numbering in the hundreds. It is not that they are raising them for profit so much as horse ownership harkens back to early days when a large herd was a sign of prestige and wealth.

It is only natural that when horsemen of any national origin get together, wagers are made as to who has the fastest horse. The Blackfeet are no exception. The race course was a level stretch of ground, free of rocks and badger holes, perhaps a mile or a mile and one-half long. A certain measured distance was not necessary. Young men, stripped to their breechclothes, were chosen to ride. They were the finest of horsemen and needed no saddle, but only a rope around the horse's jaw for a bridle. A large crowd would always gather at the finish line wagering lodges, weapons, horses, food and even women on the outcome.

At the starting place the race horses could be seen rearing and plunging, ready to be off. At a gunshot they raced away in a cloud of dust, the young riders lying low on the horses' backs, whipping their mounts unmercifully. Encouraged by the shrill cries of the spectators, they sped past the finish line amid the cheering crowd. If there was any grumbling by the loser about how the race was run, the people would pull him off his mount and rub manure on him. After bets were paid and the crowd became quiet once more, another race was arranged with other horses and riders. There are several races every day during the annual summer get-togethers.

PARADE INDIAN

We do not know what pageantry, if any, the primitive Indian had. He was probably like every other aborigine of ancient times—so busy eking out a living that he had little time for it. As their civilization advanced, the Indians required less time for basic survival and so gradually developed a culture that encouraged pageantry and ceremonial dress.

When the Spaniards arrived in the New World and moved into the interior, they were astounded at the ornate clothing and extravagant ceremonials with which the native people greeted them. The European settlers on the east coast of North America were likewise treated to impressive rituals and elaborate costuming by the natives. In various sections across the continent, the people each had their own distinct type of daily attire supplemented by more involved dress for special occasions.

Of all the costumes that the native people developed, one in particular has captured the imagination of today's public, both white and Indian: the beautiful, full-flowing eagle feather headdress of the Sioux. Nearly all of the Indians of North America, the Blackfeet included, have adopted it as their own.

It is probably safe to assume that the parade Indian as we know him today originated with the early Wild West shows of entrepreneurs such as Buffalo Bill. This is not to say that these shows developed this style of dress because the Sioux costume was showy and spectacular to begin with. Enterprising white showmen simply made great use of it, and by repeated exposure to audiences all over the world, they created that image we recognize as the American Indian dressed in full regalia, be he Sioux, Cheyenne, Blackfeet, Kiowa or Comanche!

Important Indian chieftains have met with dignitaries from every nation, and an important part of the greeting ceremonies is the granting of an Indian-sounding name and the presentation of a Sioux-style headdress. I am reminded of the time when Calvin Coolidge was presented with a bonnet. He donned his war bonnet and gratefully accepted his Indian name but didn't much look the part of an Indian chief!

I have on hand an early-day photograph of several important men of the Blackfeet tribe meeting dignitaries of Canada. Many of them are wearing the straight-up headdress while others display the split-horn bonnet. Successive photos over the years show that these were gradually replaced with the Sioux style until now the traditional Blackfeet headdress is seen only at religious functions.

Summer social get-togethers called "Indian Days" are spreading throughout the country today. Each one has its own parade of colorfully costumed Indians of both sexes and of all ages. Some of the participants are dressed in fancy dance costumes, in the traditional dress of olden days, or are costumed as in this statue of a proud Blackfeet chief mounted on his iron-grey parade horse. He is a typical parade Indian.

WAR

RETURN OF THE BLACKFEET RAIDERS

Visitors to this part of Montana often ask what the Blackfeet do for a living. If the visitor refers to present-day Blackfeet, the answer is simple; some hold jobs and work, some have ranches and businesses and others are involved in the many social programs created by our government and its Bureau of Indian Affairs.

On the other hand, if the questioner is referring to The People of the buffalo days, the answer is that they had no "occupation" as we understand the word. Other than the necessary involvement of eating, sleeping and routine camp chores, the foremost activity among the men, at least, was taking the war trail against the enemy. Telling about these deeds was one of their favorite pastimes.

A kind of rough accounting system was used in order to recognize what exploits constituted the highest honor. Deeds were rated as to the degree of danger and the amount of courage it took to perform them. Wresting a gun from a live and dangerous enemy warrior was rated as the highest coup. For instance, one of the famous old Blackfeet names was "Takes a Gun." Capturing personal effects from the enemy, such as a shield, war bonnet, war shirt, bow and arrows, tomahawk or knife rated nearly as high. Counting coup on an enemy victim probably rated next in importance because whoever counted coup on the victim could claim the scalp, even if the enemy had been killed by someone else. The taking of an ordinary horse was such a common occurrence that, although it certainly was a deed to be noted, it did not rank as high as the others, unless, of course, the horse stolen was a well-known runner or a famous war horse. War and its related activities, such as horse stealing, were the main occupations of the early Blackfeet.

The gathering of food, be it digging for roots or the gathering of berries by the women or hunting by the young men, could not be considered an occupation.

As part of the "war games," raiding after horses was the most common activity of the young men. Such forays were generally against close neighbors, but there are tales told around the lodge fires of raiders traveling as far south as the Spanish settlements where they obtained the Barbs and mustangs, and as far west as the Palouse and Nez Percé tribes who raised the big, spotted horses.

It seems that the Blackfeet seldom entered the territory of the Sioux and Mandan but targeted their raids more frequently against the Crow, Snake and Cree. Raiding parties made up of young men anxious to prove their manhood were constantly coming or going during the summer months. Horse raiding was fine fun and a thrilling activity for these adventurous young warriors. Winter usually brought an end to these raids because the raiders could be trailed too easily in the snow and also in this season most energies were directed toward simply surviving.

A bona fide war trail was not, on the other hand, a fun excursion. It was kill . . . or be killed. It was usually undertaken as a matter of revenge or to right a wrong, either real or imaginary, that had been committed by the enemy. Many times, the original reason for the

scalping raids had been forgotten. However, revenge begot revenge, and killing led to more killing. At times, the elders of both sides, realizing the futility of such a practice, would smoke the pipe for peace, and a truce would reign for a time. But sooner or later, young hotbloods of both camps would grow restless, and the scalping raids would begin as before.

The return of a victorious war party was always an occasion for rejoicing. The successful warriors would stop a short distance from camp to paint their faces and bodies and decorate the horses they were riding. At a signal, they would gallop into the camp circle singing victory songs and brandishing trophies taken from the enemy. Amid cheers from the crowd of onlookers, they would race at breakneck speed around the camp four times before dismounting. Preparation for a victory dance was sure to follow where each warrior would reenact his exploits and count his coups.

Shown in this sculpture are four Blackfeet warriors who have returned from a successful horse stealing raid on their southern enemies, the Crow. As they enter the camp singing their songs of victory, people cry out the names of each. Medicine Bull, the leader, holds aloft the war flag of the slain enemy chief; Eagle Child displays the war shirt taken from that chief; Little Wolf waves the captured war bonnet; and behind him White Antelope brandishes the slain enemy's stone-headed war club. All are mounted on horses taken from the enemy. The historical period shown is in the early 1800s, and the names of the warriors are well-known old-time Blackfeet names.

STANDING ALONE

Everything that a young man wished for—wealth, the maiden of his heart and the esteem of his peers— was to be had by successful adventures on the war trail. Sometimes the road to glory took a different turn and did not end in a triumphal return of the victor when fate decreed that he die a brave warrior's death.

When meeting a superior enemy force, the Indian warrior's philosophy generally was to escape if possible in order to live to fight again another day. If flight were impossible, he would fight like a demon. If members of a small war party were surprised by a larger enemy force in a wooded area, they would run for shelter to await nightfall, when they could escape unseen. The enemy would rarely be foolhardy enough to muster an attack on them under these conditions, regardless of the odds in their favor.

If members of a war party were surprised by a superior force out on the open prairie where little shelter was available, they would quickly dig holes and put up breastworks with rocks, dirt or whatever was at hand. On the vast prairies the enemy could be spotted at a distance so there would usually be ample time to construct adequate fortifications.

However, in broken or heavily timbered country, a surprise ambush was the rule, and the battle was usually short and bloody. If the attacking party was extremely vengeful against the Blackfeet, they would not only take scalps but also would mutilate the bodies by hacking off the hands, feet and heads of the victims. In most of these situations, the odds for success were with the enemy, so the outnumbered Blackfeet prepared to meet death as brave warriors by singing their

battle songs and by killing as many of the enemy as possible. Unlike the Dog Warrior of the Cheyenne, who, when all was lost, tied himself to a stake and fought until death, the Blackfeet stood alone and defiant to the last arrow, then fought on with knife and tomahawk. The stigma against running from an enemy made it unnecessary to tie himself in place, and he would not retreat even when the end was certain.

The Blackfeet warrior, known as the "Terror of the Northwest Plains," was feared and respected by friend and foe alike. He certainly ranked among the noblest and fiercest of the Plains warriors.

WINTER SCOUTS

In winter, when the power of Cold Maker was at its greatest and the people huddled around warming fires, they often became hard pressed for meat. Scouts were sent out to find game of any kind. Since enemy scouting parties could be on a similar mission, the scouts had to be always on the alert for danger.

This sculpture is an impressionistic treatment of two Blackfeet scouts in mid-winter, each bundled up in his Hudson Bay blanket capote and carrying a sheathed Winchester rifle.

Stories are told by the old people of hunters becoming lost in a blizzard and freezing to death. A northern blizzard can come with surprising speed, and although the Blackfeet was an observant student of nature, he would sometimes be caught out in a storm on the open prairie many miles from any protection. In such a blizzard where visibility was zero and all landmarks were obliterated, the hunter had to trust the homing instincts of his horse to take him to safety. He would see nothing until the pony stopped, and lo, there would be his lodge dimly glowing in the swirling, drifting snow.

At times, these swift killer storms forced hunters to take shelter inside the carcass of a freshly slain buffalo. When the storm let up, they would hack their way out of the frozen carcass and bring the meat home for a hungry camp. Snowbound hunters who did not come home in due time would sometimes be found inside a snow-covered buffalo carcass, frozen to death.

Straight-Up Bonnet with Boss Ribs

This style of eagle feather headdress is uniquely Blackfeet. In the early 1800s, explorer-artists Paul Kane, Karl Bodmer, and George Catlin all painted various Blackfeet chiefs wearing this type of bonnet. It differs from the now familiar Sioux style in that the feathers on the straight-up bonnet are held upright by a light buckskin thong laced inside midway up each feather. A long trailer of twenty-four feathers, representing the long dorsal or boss ribs of the buffalo, was sometimes added to it; hence the name "Straight-up Bonnet With Boss Ribs." Only very important men or great warriors were allowed to wear or could afford to own a bonnet of this sort. Being both a war and religious item, it was transferable, costing many horses and other valuables. Upon transfer of this bonnet, a certain ritual was performed, accompanied by the proper song. The new owner had to pay handsomely for this service in order to complete the transaction.

When not in use, the bonnet and trailer were dismantled and stored in separate colorfully decorated cylinders. The straight-up bonnet has gone out of style and is now worn only at special religious functions.

THE SPLIT HORN BONNET

The association between war and religion among the Blackfeet is a very close one. War-use items sometimes have religious significance, and religious items may have war-use associations. The split horn bonnet is an example of one such item. It has great power in war, and, being transferable, it may also be regarded as religious in nature. Many horses and much property is required to purchase this bonnet together with its facial painting, ceremony and song.

The split horn bonnet is so named because the horns are made of split segments of buffalo horn. The splitting is accomplished by soaking the horn in hot water until it becomes soft and then separating it lengthwise into long slender sections. While the horn strips are still soft and pliable, they are bent into the desired shape with the tips usually curved slightly outward. When the horns are fully dry, they are fastened onto a headpiece of cloth, tanned hide, or the crown of an old felt hat. To this assemblage are sewn many small pieces of white weasel fur. Colored horsehair plumes and brightly colored feathers complete the bonnet proper. Hanging from the back of the bonnet are two transverse rows of whole skins of the white weasel sewn on tanned hide or red stroud trade cloth.

The entire bonnet is heavily ochered with the red sacred paint.

Agnes Mad Plume was the owner of the Half-red Half-yellow Wrapped Split Horn Bonnet. Her bonnet, though not a true split horn bonnet, was made of rawhide strips curved in the manner of horns wrapped their entire length with red ribbons on one horn and yellow ribbons on the other. The headpiece was painted with the sacred paints, one side being yellow, the other side red. It was a ceremonial headpiece and was always worn by Agnes at the annual Indian Days parade and other festive occasions. After her death, it was bequeathed to her granddaughter, and it is she who now proudly carries on the tradition of the Mad Plume sacred headdress.

ENEMY TRACKS

A piece of freshly bent grass, an overturned stone, an empty U.S. Army canteen and the hoofprints of a shod horse tell an eloquent story to these mounted Blackfeet warriors: a member of the U.S. Cavalry, the hated Long Knives, is nearby and lost on the prairie. These warriors will make short work of this unfortunate individual when he is finally tracked down.

According to the U.S. Army, these non-conformist Indians were deemed "hostiles" to be shot on sight. They were rated as hostile because they refused to become sedentary "prisoners of war" on a certain prescribed piece of ground called a reservation. These areas, in actuality, were quite literally concentration camps. For a people who roamed at will over the vast plains asking no man where or when or if they could go, being forced to remain in any area, no matter how large, was against their very nature. These days were not good. It was a bitter war, unlike the days of raiding and coup-counting between tribes. It was far from a glamorous affair. Depredations occurred and atrocities were committed by both sides. However, "civilization" eventually won, and the proud, free warriors became stockmen, businessmen or complacent acceptors of the government dole.

THE FAST BLANKET

When a scout was sent ahead to look for the enemy, it was customary for him to ascend a prominent hill to a spot where he could be seen by his fellow warriors but not by the enemy. If the enemy were near or

approaching, he would ride his pony in a tight circle waving a blanket in a rapid circular motion. If they were far away, he would keep the pony still and wave the blanket in a slower motion.

Mirrors were sometimes used to signal, but, of course, they were of no use at dawn or dusk or if the sun was cloud-covered. Smoke signals, popularized in many a novel, were used at times. However, in the windy country of the Blackfeet, it is doubtful that this method would have been very practical.

One thing is certain, and it is that by whatever means the Plains Indian had a rapid system of communication. Nowadays we who live on the reservation have a saying that if you want a message delivered, just send it by moccasin telegraph. It will get to its destination fast and true. We do not know exactly how this is accomplished, but it definitely does happen.

When we get ready to gather in the spring to honor Thunder and unwrap His Pipe, we simply announce the date of the Opening to a few close friends, and behold, when the appointed day arrives, the meeting place is packed with people, some from as far away as four hundred miles north in Canada. This is truly remarkable because for many people who attend, modern communications systems are miles away.

A first-class war pony was priceless to the mounted warrior. He was highly trained, sure-footed, fast and unafraid of the sounds of battle.

The pony I have sculpted here is a well-built, strong animal that shows good breeding. Not one of the early Barb mustang-type horses, he perhaps was stolen from some rancher or taken from an enemy warrior toward the south. He is pictured with all of the warrior's necessary war implements—lance, shield, bow and quiver of arrows, quirt, rawhide horseshoes, rope and war club.

The saddle shown is the type known (for no apparent reason) as the Prairie Chicken Snare Saddle. It was a type commonly used by warriors when going on a journey horseback. (If the warrior was going on foot, he might carry a pad saddle, which is merely an empty bag that could be filled with grass or other padding.) The cinch was a piece of soft rawhide ingeniously fastened to it. Stirrups were made from willow or aspen covered with rawhide.

The bridle is braided rawhide with a snaffle bit and a pair of reins. The horse's tail is tied in a bun and decorated with eagle feathers. A good luck medicine charm of owl feathers is tied to the forelock. Under the horse's jaw hangs a war charm amulet which is a willow wand about sixteen inches long decorated with war eagle plumes. (A war eagle is the golden eagle, a mighty hunter; as opposed to the fish-eating, white-headed eagle.)

The horse is painted with meaningful symbols that form the warrior's protective Power. The painted designs on this war horse are those used by Gambler, an old-time warrior from the Blood Reserve in Alberta, Canada. The eyes of the horse are circled in red so that he can see at night and will not stumble in a badger's hole or fall in a grass-covered washout. Each braid in the mane ends with a tied red ribbon as a sign of war. A straight red line up the front of each foreleg is to guard against broken legs. The man design on the chest shows that an enemy had been run over on some previous war exploit. Half-circle designs on the right hip indicate enemy horses taken, and the half-square marks are for coups counted. The quarter circle with a zig-zag tail on the left hip shows participation in scouting expeditions.

The meanings of these symbols are recognized by all, but no two warriors marked their war pony in exactly the same manner. The sign of the hand, red-painted, was a common war symbol among the Plains people. Its meaning varied from tribe to tribe; among the Blackfeet it meant "I Killed an Enemy Barehanded."

61

The Price of a Scalp

In this sculpture a Crow and a Blackfeet warrior meet in deadly combat. The Blackfeet has been unhorsed, but as the Crow charges and is preparing to strike him with his war club, the Blackfeet makes one last desperate thrust with his lance and luckily pierces his enemy's heart, turning the tide of battle abruptly. Thus the price the Crow warrior has paid for attempting to take the scalp of a Blackfeet enemy is the forfeiture of his own life.

Intertribal warfare in the early days was common. Many times the war parties were small and actually did little serious damage. After a scalp or two had been taken, the party would return home to have a victory celebration and to publicly count their coups. At times, however, large groups of warriors would assemble to make an all-out attack on an enemy encampment. One such battle, between Assiniboin-Cree and the Piegan (Blackfeet), occurred at Fort McKenzie at the confluence of the Missouri and the Marias rivers, August 28, 1833. Being an eyewitness to the encounter, Karl Bodmer executed a brilliant drawing of the event.

In 1870 the last great battle between tribes on the Northern Plains took place in Canada near present-day Lethbridge, Alberta. Between two and three hundred warriors lost their lives. This battle was again between the Cree and the Blackfeet—archenemies since antiquity.

To Take a Scalp

The custom of taking parts of the body from an enemy has been practiced since the beginning of the story of man. These were taken to be worn as fetishes or as signs to others that the wearers had indeed killed. During the French and Indian Wars the opposing British and French forces paid to have their enemies destroyed. Each side used Indian scouts and warriors to prey on the other. In order to collect the bounty, scouts would bring evidence in the form of a scalp or both ears. On the Western frontier redmen and whitemen alike continued the practice.

Nowadays, we look upon this practice as repugnant and barbaric, but it was part of a very real and valid way of life in the early days on the frontier. In the early nineteenth century, artists Karl Bodmer, George Catlin and Paul Kane all reported seeing freshly taken scalps in the Indian camps they visited. Their paintings of human scalp-lock apparel worn by the Blackfeet and other tribes are visual proof of this practice.

Some victims survived their scalping. Prince Maximilian saw people among the Blackfeet who had been scalped and covered their heads with little caps.

Nearly everyone has a morbid curiosity about how this grisly task was accomplished. Hence, I created this sculpture to illustrate at least one way it was done. The Crow has fallen face down with an arrow in his side. The victorious Blackfeet places his left foot between the shoulder blades of the victim. The hair was usually done up in three braids—one on either side of the head, and a third, the scalp-lock, hanging down the back. The victor grabs the scalp-lock and with a deft motion encircles the skull with his sharp knife. After several slices to loosen the skin, he lifts the dripping bloody trophy from the enemy's skull!

One method of preserving the scalp was to scrape the skin side clean and then lace it on a small willow hoop where it was allowed to dry thoroughly. After it was properly cured, the skin side was either covered with trade cloth and decorated with beads or simply painted with red ochre. A slender willow wand was attached so that it could be held while dancing. Sometimes the scalp was tied to spear shafts or gun barrels. When used to ornament buckskin shirts and leggings, hair-locks without the skin were used.

End of the War Trail

Along the major rivers in Blackfeet country are great groves of cottonwood trees. Burial in these trees was commonplace in the early days. I know of two such burial trees that are still standing. One site was that of a child near Starr School, north of Browning, and the other was that of the Indian wife of James Willard Schultz near the Holy Family Mission, south of Browning on the Two Medicine River. The burial date of the child was probably about 1950. That of the woman was 1903.

Burials were also in caves along the steep cliffs and on high hills where the bodies were covered over with rocks as protection against wolves and coyotes. Sometimes a death tipi was used. Half-buried circles of rocks marking an ancient tipi burial site can still be found in isolated spots on the top of prominent hills.

During the later reservation period of 1890 to 1920, burials were made in small log or board houses. With the coming of ever stricter government controls, these above-ground graves were not permitted. Yet the religious beliefs of the early Blackfeet were strong, and it was only with great difficulty that the law concerning underground burial was enforced.

The Blackfeet did not have a cheerful outlook for an after-death life. They be-

lieved that the spirit journeyed eastward to the Sand Hills—a dreary place—where its existence was similar to the one it had when the person was alive. They also believed that quicksands prevented the living from entering. However, the spirits could roam at will, and it was thought that they could communicate with the living any time they chose to, as long as it was at night.

As shown in this sculpture, the dead were sometimes placed upon scaffolds built in trees. They were dressed in their finest and provided with all the articles needed for the journey to the Sand Hills. A warrior would need his pipe, weapons, horse gear, drum and other personal items that he valued. His favorite horse might be killed so that he could have it to chase the spirit buffalo.

The practice of self-mutilation for a deceased loved one was common in the early days. Here is shown a young widow mourning the death of her warrior-husband. She is cutting her hair, slashing her arms and legs, and wailing, wailing, wailing; a heart-rending sound for anyone who has ever heard it. The bereaved one has been known to bleed to death on the spot. Some have even thrown themselves over high cliffs onto rocks below to join their loved ones in death.

CONTACT WITH THE WHITE MAN

HE-THAT-LOOKS-AT THE-CALF MEETS
CAPTAIN LEWIS

One of the most incredible journeys ever undertaken by the American military was that carried out by the Corps of Discovery, the Lewis and Clark Expedition, when it explored up the Missouri River and on to the West Coast and back from 1804-1806.

It opened to settlement and eventual development the vast unexplored Northwest Territory and helped establish ownership of lands claimed by both Great Britain and the fledgling United States. One of the remarkable things about the journey into this wild and unknown territory was that not one member was lost due to hostile tribesmen, wild animals or other pitfalls along the trail. (True, one member of the expedition,

Sergeant Floyd, died early into the journey but due to natural causes, possibly a ruptured appendix.)

Although the Sioux gave the expedition some anxious moments on the outgoing journey, they were overcome by a show of strength from the captains. But on the return trip it was the Blackfeet who nearly put an end to the entire mission! After wintering on the West Coast, the expedition returned in 1806. When they had made their way back through the Rockies, the expedition was split into two groups: Captain Clark set out to explore the headwaters of the Yellowstone River with twenty men; Captain Lewis struck out for the great falls of the Missouri with nine men to pick up the contents of the caches they had left on the way west.

Four men—Captain Lewis, Reuben Fields, Joseph Fields and George Drouillard—split from the rest of that party at the falls and headed north to investigate

The party was beset by wet, miserable weather, so after remaining there several days taking notes and various readings of latitude and longitude, they broke camp and headed in a southeasterly direction toward a high knoll visible in the distance. They were in the midst of unknown country with perhaps ten or twelve thousand unfriendly Indians roaming the area. A lone cow buffalo with a Blackfeet arrow sticking in its side gave evidence of the proximity of hostiles.

As the four men approached a river, Drouillard chose the north side to hunt for deer while Captain Lewis with Joseph and Reuben Fields went on to ascend the hill on the south side. They had just reached the crest when off to the east at quite some distance they spied an Indian war party. There appeared to be a large number, but upon glassing the group, Lewis made out only eight warriors with a band of stolen horses. The warriors were so intent on watching Drouillard on the far side of the river that they failed to spot Lewis and his two men right away. But when they did, they hurriedly prepared for battle. One of their number, He-That-Looks-At-The-Calf, raced over on his war pony to accost the group of strangers (See Thwaites, ed., *Original Journals of the Lewis and Clark Expedition,* Volume V). This sculpture depicts that tension-filled moment.

An interesting and historically important anecdote is that after some parlay, Captain Lewis and his men decided to make camp with the Blackfeet. The camp was made near the river under three cottonwood trees. (This spot has been located, and the three trees are still standing. An historical plaque marks this place, too.) Early in the morning a movement was felt by the lightly dozing Joseph Fields; his gun was being slipped from his hand! He shouted a warning, and the camp came alive. Two Indians had taken guns, and the rest were making off with the horses! The Blackfeet who had stolen Joseph's gun was chased down and killed; the one who had taken Lewis' gun was shot and wounded by Lewis and later died. From stories handed down through the years by the Blackfeet, that warrior was He-That-Looks-At-The-Calf. It was during this melee that the expedition and its leader nearly came to an end, for as Lewis states in his journal, "being bearheaded, I felt the wind of his bullet very distinctly." Fearful that the Indians would return in force, Lewis and his men rode southeast in great haste. This was the only incident of its kind to happen on the great journey and regretfully, it involved the Blackfeet. Many long years of mutual suspicion and warfare followed before the Americans were allowed to come into Blackfeet country.

the headwaters of the Marias River. The territory that this river drained would establish the land claim of the United States, according to the provisions of the Louisiana Purchase. This was one of the major objectives of the expedition.

The four explorers made their way without incident but with much apprehension through the Blackfeet country. They traveled up the Marias and on up Cut Bank Creek about nine miles northeast of the present site of the town of Browning. Noting that they had reached the farthest north point of the creek, they stopped and made camp. (An historical plaque now marks the spot.) Captain Lewis called it Camp Disappointment because of the fact that the drainage did not originate farther north, thus enabling the United States to lay claim to additional territory as President Jefferson had hoped.

TRADE GOODS

A culture can exist for many years with little apparent change when not subjected to outside influences. However, let elements of a different culture be introduced, and soon thereafter the new replaces the old and becomes so entrenched that it would seem impossible to continue without it. For instance, if a primitive people who have used stone and bone implements for thousands of years are exposed to steel tools, the old implements are thrown aside for the new, and the people not only become dependent on the introduced item but also upon the supplier of that item. Hence, the trader is born!

People in the Western Hemisphere were actually exposed to foreign influence hundreds of years ago, but the impact of these first voyagers to the New World left little impression. However, it was not until the late 1400s that other voyagers came and did make a lasting impression on the people of the New World. These were the Spaniards who introduced new weaponry, metal tools and a new religious concept. Yet to the people of the Great Plains, the introduction of the horse, together with the bridle, saddle and stirrup, was the cause of the greatest change in their old ways.

As the Europeans spread over the continent, the native people became more

and more dependent upon material goods such as beads, cloth, weapons, cooking utensils, blankets. In turn, the furs that the natives caught were much in demand in Europe so a brisk trade flourished. High crown beaver hats, which were very much in vogue in Europe and the eastern United States, put the beaver pelt high on the list of valuable furs.

There was also a lively market for the soft, silky fur hides of winter-killed cow buffalo which were used as lap robes in the carriage trade. And, more importantly, as the Industrial Revolution developed along the eastern seaboard, the demand for cheap, heavy leather for belting and harnesses increased, and with the demand came hide hunters and the eventual destruction of the immense herds of buffalo and the near extinction of this species.

I have shown no whiskey being traded in this sculpture because I detest what it has done to a proud and vigorous race. Nevertheless, it was one of the primary items of exchange. The whiskey trade created a sordid chapter in the history of the West. By weakening the resistance of these warrior-people, it certainly had a great deal to do with the opening of the West to "civilization."

RELIGION

Onesta and the Sacred Bear Spear

Onesta was the owner of the Sacred Bear Spear. There were many rules governing its care because the spear was a transferable religious object as well as a weapon of war. For instance, when moving camp, the Spear was never allowed to lie on the ground. Instead, it was hung on a tripod until it and its bundle could be placed on the Sacred Horse that was provided for its transport. At the new camp it was placed on a special tripod behind the lodge. It was carried outside at sunup and inside at sundown and remained inside on stormy days. Being a man's spear, it could not be touched by women. Sweetgrass and the root of the holy turnip were used as incense beneath the Spear. The Bear Spear was dismantled in late autumn when the bears retired for the winter and unrolled and taken out in the spring when they came out of their winter dens.

As is the case with all sacred objects among the Blackfeet, the Bear Spear has an origin myth. Briefly told, the story is as follows. After a journey, a certain dog and its travois, owned by an important chief, turned up missing when The People arrived at the new camping place. There were many valuables packed on the travois, so a band of warriors immediately set out to search the previous campsite for it. They saw no sign of the missing dog, the travois or any of the items that were packed on it. They returned to camp and reported their lack of success to the chief.

Now, the chief's young son, Sa-ko-ma-pi, begged to go alone to try to find the dog and its travois. With reluctance, knowing that his son was undertaking an exceedingly dangerous mission, his father finally granted permission. Sa-ko-ma-pi first went to the old campground and found the place where their tipi had stood. He searched the ground for "sign" in ever widening circles until he finally found a dim travois track leading off into the thick underbrush. Using extreme caution, he followed the ever-so-faint trail which led him to a cave where he found the missing travois and all its valuables, but no dog.

Suddenly, a huge grizzly appeared. The boy was so frightened that he could neither speak nor move. It is said by The People that in the long ago men and animals could talk to one another in a common language. Thus the bear spoke to the boy. "I am Medicine Grizzly. I will do you no harm. It is time for winter sleep. You must spend this time with me in my warm den." Not wishing to offend the grizzly, Sa-ko-ma-pi felt he had to accept the invitation. When Spring finally came and it was time to leave the cave, the bear returned the travois along with all the valuables.

He also bestowed upon the boy his supernatural Power by showing him how to make the Bear Spear. Fetching a long stick, he told Sa-ko-ma-pi, "Put a point on this and tie it well. Cover the staff with strips of Real Bear's skin and tie a Real Bear's jaws, claws and nose on it. You will then paint the entire spear with the sacred red paint." He also told the boy, "Draw a black line across your forehead and two curved lines at either side of your mouth to represent a bear's tusks and use the sacred red paint all over your body. A grizzly claw you will tie in your hair, and when you go into battle, you must carry the Spear high toward the enemy while singing the Bear Song. My supernatural Power will go with you when you charge the enemy roaring like a Real Bear. Then the enemy will surely run from you."

Sa-ko-ma-pi returned home amid much rejoicing and made the spear as Medicine Grizzly had instructed him. Not long afterward, the Blackfeet and the Crow met in a great battle. The boy, carrying the Sacred Bear Spear, led the attack, and the Crows were put to flight. The Blackfeet killed many of the enemy and won the battle. Sa-ko-ma-pi was made a war chief, and from thenceforward The People respected the Bear Spear as having Supernatural Powers. The Power of the Spear was not only used in battle but also its great powers were used to heal the sick. Until recently this spear was in the archives at the Museum of the Plains Indian, Browning.

The Holy Woman

At the gathering of The People for the great annual summer camp Holy Bundles are opened, and the transfer of ownership of many religious items takes place. There is gambling, visiting and horse racing. It is a grand social time, but by far the most important event is the Okan with all its attendant activities including the raising of the Great Lodge to Sun. "Spoo moe kit, Nah too si" (Help us, Oh Sun) is an oft-repeated cry heard throughout the camp during these days.

Only a pure and virtuous woman would dare to make the Sacred Vow to Sun, but when someone very

dear to her was in great danger—suffering from a serious illness, for example, or out on the war trail—some woman would promise to put up a lodge to Sun and eat of the Sacred Food in the Moon of Ripening Berries. The promise to become The Holy Woman was a very serious undertaking fraught with superstitious dread. If the sick one died or the one on the war trail met with disaster, she would be deemed as having been unworthy and be forever shunned. Even the others who agreed to help her would share in her guilt should any bad things occur. Hers was a heavy burden.

In the olden days when The People were hunters of buffalo, the man and his woman who had pledged to give the Sun Dance would collect from donors all the buffalo tongues and sarvis berries needed for the sacred feast. They took no active part in the hunting of buffalo or in collecting the ripened berries; that was done by others who wished to gain special favor. The Holy Woman of the previous year and her husband were on hand at all times to teach the rituals to the new Holy Woman. The sacred Natoas headdress that she was to wear had been purchased from the former owner at a handsome price of many horses, blankets and other items. The former owner and her husband were also paid for their instructions to the initiate.

Shown in this sculpture is the procession of Holy People moving from the fasting lodge to the receiving lodge. Their path is laid with blankets and robes given to them by people who wished special prayers. Leading this group is the Holy Man from the previous year. Next comes the new Holy Woman, wearing the Holy Natoas headdress and the Sacred Elk Skin Robe, her face showing the effects of four days of fasting. The Holy Turnip Digging Stick is tied on her back. Everything is red-painted, symbolizing the Morning Star myth. Following her is the Holy Woman of the previous year, then the new Holy Woman's husband, and finally an assistant or friend of the initiate.

The Holy Woman is the most revered of all The People, and the Natoas Bundle, while small in size compared to the Medicine Pipe Bundle and the huge Beaver Bundle, is the most sacred of all bundles.

A WARRIOR'S VOW

While on the war trail a warrior sometimes made a vow to Natosi (Sun) that if he was successful in his exploits and lived to return to his people he would perform the self-torture ritual at the next Okan and raising of the Lodge to Sun. He told others of his vow so that he would not be able to break his promise, because to do so would certainly have brought disgrace to him and all his relatives.

In due course, the time came for holding the Okan and for the building of the Sacred Lodge, and the warrior prepared for his ordeal. After many days of fasting and partaking of the holy sweat bath, he was ready. Thenceforth no food or water was allowed to pass his lips. He painted his body and face in the proper manner and tied the holy sage around his head and about his wrists.

He was now ready for his helpers to make the incisions for the sticks; two parallel vertical slits were made on each side of the chest above the nipples. A curious custom was that when the cuts were made, he was asked whether he wanted them made thick or thin. The cutters usually did just the opposite, so a really brave man would say cut them thin. Short, stout sticks were passed through each slit. Thongs suspended from near the top of the center pole of the Sun Lodge were tied firmly to the sticks. As added penance, a war shield was tied with thongs through slits cut over his shoulder blades. On rare occasions, the skull of a freshly killed buffalo bull was used in place of the war shield.

He had to exert all the power at his command to strain against the incisions on his breast until the flesh tore loose, and he fell to the ground. If the warrior was unsuccessful, his helpers would leap on him and with their added weight cause the flesh to rip apart. Then the young man ran with the article on his back and if it failed to rip out, helpers again added their weight to tear it loose.

The ritual vow to Sun was not to be taken lightly. Some died of shock or infection after their ordeal. Few men alive today have endured it. One warrior who had undergone the Sun Ceremony and was still living when I was a boy was Heavy Head from the Blood Reserve in Canada. Another was Green-Grass-Bull, who lived in Browning and in later years of his life hauled water from Willow Creek for use by the local housewives in doing their laundry. Little did I know or even dream at the time that this man had once been a great warrior and had made this sacrifice to Sun because of his beliefs. He was known only as the man with twenty-five dogs: "There goes old Green-Grass-Bull and his dogs."

The government put a stop to this ritual of self-torture in 1894, but today there are whispers that some young men believe in Sun Power enough to again perform this ritual.

OPENING OF THE THUNDER MEDICINE PIPE

The Blackfeet believe that Thunder (not lightning) was one of the mightiest manifestations of the All Powerful One. They say that at the beginning of the world Thunder gave the decorated stem of his pipe and all of the items that accompany it to a man and his woman for safekeeping, bidding them to wrap it carefully, smudge it daily with the scent of the sweet pine and in other ways guard its well-being. Thunder reserved the pipe bowl for himself to be used only on very special occasions. He promised the man and his wife that when he returned in the Spring, he would announce his coming with a loud voice that would shake the Heavens and make the whole earth tremble. At that time, they must call all The People together and in a certain prescribed ceremony unwrap the Pipe Stem. The man was to dance with it, and the woman would stand up, thus showing to Thunder and all The People that they had fulfilled their obligation.

It was perceived by others that The Keeper of the Pipe Stem had uncommonly good fortune, so it seemed to them that the Power of the Pipe was strong and they longed to share it. In time, others were granted permission to construct Thunder Pipes but always according to a rigid formula handed down by Tailfeathers Woman and Scarface, rules which had been given to them by Sun in the long ago. While each Pipe was similar to the others, there were individual variations that gave special Powers to its owner. All the Thunder Pipes now in existence are known by certain specific names such as Long Time Pipe, Backside To The Fire Pipe and Arapaho Pipe.

There are two parts to the ritual opening of a Pipe Bundle. The first part of the ceremony involves all the prayers and songs necessary to unwrap the Holy Bundle and its contents. This part is followed by a feast of sacred berry soup, fry bread, boiled ribs, and coffee or tea. The second part of the opening is for all Pipe owners and others who are authorized to dance with The Pipe or other bundle parts (such as the Owl, Rattle, Tongs, Woman's Pipestem) to receive that item's Power. It is also a time for others to receive special blessings from the Pipe. The Pipe Bundle

ceremony ends with the ritual planting of tobacco seeds and the passing out of smoking tobacco as a gift from the Pipe owner.

The ceremony, conducted entirely from memory, has changed over the years so that a Pipe Opening of today is a condensed version of the ancient ritual. However, the Power of the Pipe is strong and for believers the basic religious meaning and sincerity of feeling remain as always.

The Thunder Pipe ceremony may be likened to the fertility rites of other primitive peoples. The welcoming back of the spring rains, the return of the migratory birds, the symbolic planting of the tobacco plants and the sarvis berry—all are reenactments of the rites of spring.

There are several Medicine Pipes still in existence among the Blackfeet, and each Pipe is opened with the proper ceremony at least once a year. The opening of these various Pipes is one of the most important religious occasions of The People. There are less than a dozen Holy Men who have the knowledge to conduct the ceremony in the traditional manner, and they are becoming fewer with each passing year. Some of the younger men are trying to learn, but it seems doubtful that this can be accomplished. When the last shaman leaves this earth for the Sand Hills, the Thunder Medicine Pipe as an active religious ceremony of the Blackfeet will cease to exist. However—who knows—perhaps the Power of the ancient Pipe will somehow be able to survive and continue to be a force for good in our world.

DANCE OF THE BEAVER WOMEN

The myths are many regarding the creation of the Beaver Bundle, the largest and the oldest of all the sacred Bundles of the Blackfeet. While stories of its origin vary greatly, it is certain that this bundle is uniquely theirs. Some anthropologists believe that it grew to its present great size and complexity by the whims of powerful medicine men who, when they became aware of a new bundle that apparently had great Power, would claim it for incorporation into their Beaver Bundles. It became a composite that included the Tobacco Planting Ritual, the Calling of the Buffalo Ritual, the Sun Dance Ritual and some

ceremonies of the Medicine Pipe. It also came to include songs and descriptive dances of nearly all of the birds and animals known to the Blackfeet. Eventually there were three or four hundred songs to be sung, plus all of the proper prayers and dances.

Although the Bundle was owned by just one man and his wife, they were never able to learn the entire ritual alone, so they employed several specialists to help with the ceremonies. The intelligence and memory required for the opening of a Beaver Bundle was incredible. The Holy Men were always fearful of committing errors—or bad luck would certainly befall everyone.

During my lifetime the number of Beaver men and women has dwindled so that now there are not enough remaining to perform the ceremony, and as a consequence the Beaver Bundle as a living religious rite is virtually extinct. In 1972, a member of the Blood Indian Band in Canada by the name of Calling Last transferred his Beaver Bundle to a Canadian ethnologist. A documentary movie with sound was made at the time under the auspices of the Alberta Government Provincial Museum and is now in the museum's archives. This was the last known ceremonial opening of a Beaver Bundle.

Even though the Bundle is owned by only one man and his wife, various items in it could be purchased by other individuals who wished to share in the Power. When the time came in the ceremony to sing the song of or dance with the item they owned, they participated in that particular part. All of the people shown in this sculpture have in some manner shared in this Bundle that is being opened. They have either owned certain items or are past owners of an item in other Beaver Bundles. Various facial paintings signify an individual's relationship to the Bundle. Some of the participants have certain Society facial paintings, others have been granted the facial painting of this owner and still others have individual dream-given designs.

Part of the ritual includes dancing the Dance of the Beaver, which is performed by women who are wives of Beaver Men. Holding beaver-chewed sticks in their mouths and carrying a stuffed beaver skin, they imitate it swimming and going in and out of its lodge. That part of the ceremony is shown in this sculpture. The singers are older men who know all of the songs that are required. Instead of drums, rattles made from the scrotum of the bull buffalo are used. They are struck on a piece of buffalo rawhide positioned on the ground in front of the singers. Red-ochred rawhide is painted with Frog, Lizard and Snake symbols.

Of all the animals, Frog, Lizard and Snake are the only ones whose skins are not in the Bundle and the only ones who do not have a song. The reason their skins are not in the Bundle is that their skins are so very thin they would dry up to nothing and be of no use in the ceremony; and, because they could sing no song, the three mutually agreed that they would be represented by having their pictures painted on the rawhide drums where the Beaver Men would beat their rattles. Besides the three aforementioned animals, Mountain Sheep, Lion and Owl are not represented in the Bundle by songs.

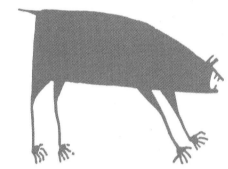

MYTHOLOGY

The Story of Miscinskee

Little Badger

A young man had a dream vision. He was riding his favorite white pony in the area of the Valley of the Medicine Grizzly (Cut Bank Canyon) when he saw two striped squirrels playing in the grass. He got off his horse to catch them, and at that very moment a half-grown badger came out of a hole hissing loudly. He told the young man to get back on his horse and stay there until he finished a job he had to do. After much pulling and tugging, the little badger finally dragged a large piece of moose hide out of the hole and up to his home on the hill. The boy did help him, however, by warding off the attacks of a big, black-colored animal and several black-colored birds, who were trying to take the hide.

Miscinskee (Little Badger) then told the boy this, "You have done me a favor by keeping these bad animals and birds away while I worked, so to show my thanks I give you my sacred dream-painted lodge. It is yours, and here is the way it must be painted. The mountain hills at the bottom of the lodge will be red, as Sun colors them when He arrives with first light. Two discs of black will be on each hill, one above the other, to represent the hole I came out of and the one I went into.

"The main part of the lodge will be yellow, the color of leaves in the Berry Moon. A great circle of blue must be painted on the back of the lodge and another on the front around the door opening, this to represent the sky when I look out of my hole. On the large yellow painted area you must make a likeness of me. Two figures on the south side and two on the north side should point in opposite directions as though I was entering these great circles.

"Running from the bottom of the lodge to the top at the back and at the front, you must paint the thirteen stripes and the dots the color of the prairie striped squirrel. Near the top of the lodge there will be painted four horizontal black stripes; those on the north to represent four black-furred animals, and those on the south to represent four black-feathered birds. The top of the lodge will be black to represent the night sky. On the smoke flaps you will paint the Seven Stars (Big Dipper) on the north side, and the Bunched Stars (Pleiades) on the south. That is the way you shall paint the lodge I have given you. I will tell you how to make the Bundle that goes with the lodge, the prayers, song, facial markings and the smudge (incense) that accompany it when it is transferred, but not until you have

made the lodge cover will I do all this. Un-yuh, I have spoken."

This is a true story of the creation of a new dream-painted tipi. The lodge has been accepted into the great camp circle by The People. The entire ceremony was recorded by anthropologists, the news media and a group from the Montana Historical Society and was witnessed by several respected non-Indian persons. The ceremony consisted of the painting of the lodge skin, a Medicine Pipe ceremony and the actual dedication of the lodge where the prayers and the blessings of The People were received, followed by a great feast for all.

Tailfeathers Woman and Morning Star

Tailfeathers Woman was young and very beautiful. Many of the young men wanted to marry her, but she refused them all. Her sisters would make jokes to her about which one of the braves she was going to marry, but she would laughingly point to the Morning Star shining brightly in the sky and say, "Some day I will marry that one."

One day as she was going to fetch water and dig turnips, an extremely handsome young man dressed in the finest of white buckskin appeared on the trail and said, "I am Morning Star, and I have come to take you for my woman." At first she was surprised and so refused him, but remembering her promise, she agreed to join Him. Taking her by the hand, He led her up to the heavens where His father, Sun, and His mother, Moon, lived. Their lodge was beautiful, and she was very happy.

One of the duties of the women was to dig the edible root of the prairie turnip. A long, pointed stick with a large knob on one end, the turnip-digging stick, was used for this purpose. Tailfeathers Woman had brought her own stick with her, as each woman used her own. Morning Star told her to go dig some turnips while He was away on His journey around the heavens but cautioned her not to dig a certain large one that He pointed out.

Of course, when He had gone, she could not resist the temptation to find out why she should not dig that one. After some hesitation, she finally dug the large

turnip; it made a hole in the sky! Some call it the North Star, but The People know that the hole in the sky was made by Tailfeathers Woman. When she looked down, she saw the buffalo, the mountains, the lodges and her people, and she began to cry from loneliness. When Morning Star returned, she told Him what she had done and that she wanted to go home. At first, He was very angry, but after a while He pitied her and agreed that she should be sent back to Earth. Now, as it happened, Morning Star and Tailfeathers Woman had a son, so arrangements were made to lower the mother and son down the hole to her people. With a strong spider web tied onto them, they were let down through the hole where the turnip had been.

SCARFACE

Scarface, a long-ago ancestor of the Blackfeet, is credited with giving them the concept of Sun as the most important symbol of the Creator. Legend has it that in the long ago, a poor young man with a deep ugly scar on his face desired a beautiful young girl for his woman. She jokingly replied that, if he rid his face of the scar and performed some great deed, she would agree to marry him.

Scarface set out on his quest. He met and talked with many animals and birds on his travels; none could help him but all agreed that he should keep

traveling toward the West. Finally, he came to the edge of a huge body of water where he met two large white birds who said that they could take him to an island out in the water where the Great One lived. This they did, and when he got there, he met Sun, the Great One, and his wife, Night Red Light (Moon), and their son, Early Riser (Morning Star). Scarface told them of his quest, and after learning of some of his harrowing experiences, they took pity on him. They grew to love the boy, and he and Early Riser became as brothers.

The two were warned that when they wandered about the island they were not to go near a certain flock of huge deadly birds. These birds had killed all of Early Riser's brothers and would now try to kill Him.

One day when the Great One and Night Red Light were away on their daily journey, the boys could not resist the temptation to go hunting for the forbidden birds. Upon seeing the boys, the birds immediately attacked. Scarface intervened in Early Riser's defense and with his spear killed all seven of the terrible birds. Upon Sun's return from His journey, He was extremely pleased that all of the long-billed killers had been slain. As a reward, Sun offered to remove Scarface's deformity. To further show His gratitude, Sun, ruler of the Heaven and Earth, gave the secrets of His great Sun Lodge to Scarface so that all The People might have long life, health and happiness. Sun bade farewell to the now handsome young man and showed him the short way home down the Wolves' Trail (the Milky Way).

The People practice the annual observance to Sun to this very day and reenact the ceremonies in the manner set down by Scarface in the long ago. There are many versions of this legend—this is only one of them.

The Seven Faces of Scarface in this mythical sculpture shows the gradual removal of the scars—one for each of the seven killer birds that were slain. Eventually, the faces of Scarface and Early Riser became identical. Even now, at the first light of dawn, one can see two stars shining ever so brightly; one, the true Morning Star and the other the false Morning Star, said by many to be Early Riser and His friend Scarface.

THE RAVEN SPEAKS

Of utmost importance in the making of a Blackfeet warrior was his vision quest. In this search for a spiritual helper, he would travel many days until, guided by intuition or the spirits, he would find a place of utter solitude where the Above Ones might communicate with him. Days and nights of fasting followed. Though they would push themselves to the limits of endurance, not all aspiring young warriors were successful. Some made several attempts only to receive no vision at all. But others were rewarded with a vision of their dream helper and thereby gained a strong medicine. Medicine in this sense means Religious Strength, Inner Strength or Spiritual Power.

All animals and birds as well as natural objects were potential "Vision Givers," with Eagle and Raven being among the strongest and most powerful of these figures. The smartest of all fliers, Raven is strong and can see food far, far away so he never goes hungry, and unlike most birds he is present in winter as well as in summer so he is always ready to give help in any season.

Shown in this sculpture is a Great Raven bringing in his beak the bundle and staff of the Raven Carrier Society. He will give the vision seeker the staff and all of the Supernatural Power it embodies. Raven will show him the movements of the ceremonial dance and the manner of facial and body painting together with the song. The Raven Carrier Society has great powers to heal the sick and injured.

THE BEAVER LOVER

There are few people in the world today who still live in the immediate vicinity of the origin of one of their most important rituals. The Blackfeet are one of these fortunate people. The concept and myth of the Beaver Bundle occurred in the dim past at what The People call the Inside Lakes or Lakes Inside. This lovely country is now known as Upper and Lower St. Mary's Lakes. The Upper Lake, one of the most breathtakingly beautiful lakes in the world, is in Glacier National Park and is surrounded on three sides by mountains reaching into the heavens. The Lower Lake rests entirely within the boundaries of the Blackfeet Reservation.

There are several stories concerning the origin of the Beaver Bundle. This sculpture is my impressionistic treatment of one of these myths, which was told to me by Reuben Black Boy, an elderly Blackfeet. According to him, the story is that a young man and his wife were camped on the Lower Inside Lake in the summer of long ago. The man would go out every day for camp meat. As the days went by, he began to notice a change in his young wife's attitude toward him. Since there was no camp within several Suns, he became very curious as to what was going on.

So one day he bid his wife adieu, and going only a short distance from camp, he sat down to wait. After a while, he cautiously made his way back. He crept forward, parted the bushes and was astonished at what he saw. His young wife and a huge beaver were making love. The man gave a great shout and rushed the two lovers with his knife drawn, ready to kill. The beaver, who was chief of all the beavers, asked the man to have pity on him and promised that if his life were spared, he would give the man his all-powerful Secret Bundle of the Beaver People, which would enable him to become a great chief and also the most powerful Holy Man of his tribe.

The man accepted the proposition and began to learn the ritual. The Bundle of the Beaver was a large one, as it included the skin or parts of all the birds and animals that The People knew about. With each one, a song was sung or a prayer was uttered. It took the man a long time to learn everything, so by the time he was ready to take over the huge Bundle, a beaver child was born.

As time went on, certain other ceremonies and Power items were added. It could be used to call the buffalo and also to help people recover from sickness or to protect them from danger. Counting sticks were placed in the Bundle, and the man was given the privilege of being the counter of the moons and the record-keeper. The seeds of the sacred tobacco were kept in the security of the Bundle, and even the Natoas is said to have been kept there in the early days.

SECRETS OF THE NIGHT

The owl is mentioned frequently in Blackfeet lore, generally as a harbinger of ill omen. Of all the creatures of the wild, Owl knows most about the goings-on of the Night People. With his huge yellow eyes, he sees everything both in daylight and in the dark of night; with his extra large ear openings, he can hear the rustle of a mouse running in the grass; and with his soft feathered wings, his flight is practically soundless. Owls are thought to be the ghosts of Medicine Men and thus are regarded as fearful birds. When they speak, The People heed their message. It is believed that they can foretell the approach of enemy war parties and that they have foreknowledge of great sickness or other disasters, even death. Therefore, The People have a superstitious dread of Owl.

If a warrior has the wing of an owl among his Holy things, he has the Power to take horses from the enemy at night. However, he must sing the Owl song which is,

"The night is my medicine. I hoot."

It is believed by many that the owner of an owl amulet must never be struck with a moccasin or else he would be wounded in that spot. All other places would be invulnerable.

When the owner of an owl amulet goes on the warpath, he must paint his face yellow all over and dot it with blue to represent the owl's face. The song to be sung by the warrior is, "I (the owl) am looking for something to eat, an enemy or a horse."

This sculpture shows a young brave night herding the pony herd of The People, listening attentively to the message that See-pis-too (Owl) brings.

It seems strange to me that the owl, regarded as it is by The People, is used in so many of their ceremonies and in other ways. Owl feathers are tied to the forelock of the war pony; and they are included in the amulets of warriors. I have seen arrows fletched with owl feathers. Furthermore, the owl skin is danced with at the Medicine Pipe ceremony having its own song and dance. Still, I have found The People very reluctant to talk about him, and they show genuine apprehension when asked about Owl.

NAPI TEACHES THEM THE DANCE

Napi (Old Man) occupies a rather unique position in the mythology of the Blackfeet. Although he was credited with creating the ground, the mountains, rivers, lakes and all manner of living things, he was not rated as a god and was never prayed to as such.

Old Man was always hungry so when he saw a bunch of elk on a far hillside, his thoughts were of how he could satisfy the growlings in his stomach. After much careful consideration, he thought the best approach was to walk directly across the valley toward the elk. As he proceeded, he noticed a steep bluff. "Kiy-yo," he muttered to himself. "I will coax them down to this place and get them to jump over. And they will all be killed in the same way as I showed The People how to get many of the Ee-nee (the buffalo).

He finally reached the elk, and walking with a stick and limping, he got their attention and their sympathy and said: "Oh, my elk brothers, I am tired and lame, and I need some help to cross this big valley." They took pity on him and so the herd bull elk said, "Go ahead, Old Man, and we will all help you." Old Man knew he had them fooled and so led them as he limped along over this hill and through that valley for a long time.

When Sun had gone to sleep and everything was

dark, he led them to the drop off at the bluff. Then he sneaked off and ran around one side of the bluff where there was a gradual slope and placing himself right under the drop off place, he hollered up to the elk, "Come on, this is a nice place to come down. I have come down easily with only my walking stick to help. It is a nice jump—you will all laugh."

The elk had by now gotten to trust Old Man so they all jumped off and were killed except for one cow elk. Old Man coaxed and coaxed but she would not jump. "Have pity on me," said the cow elk. "I am heavy with calf—he is about to be born. So I am afraid to jump."

"I will pity you then," answered Old Man. "You need not jump—just go ahead and live. Because of your being heavy with calf, there will always be lots of elk forever."

The next day after the elk were skinned and the meat was cut into thin slices for dry meat, the tongues were taken from the elk heads and put up on a pole to dry. Old Man then made a fire and cooked elk ribs for a good feast. The following day he went out looking around the country. He threw away his walking stick because he really wasn't limping anyway, and as he walked his thoughts kept coming back to all the rich dried elk meat and tongues that were awaiting him at his camp.

"I'll cook more of those juicy ribs tonight," he muttered to himself as he headed back. "And the marrow gut will be stuffed and cooked, and I'll have some boiled tongue. Ah ha, I will feast well again tonight."

When he got back to the place, he looked around; the meat was all gone! Wolves and coyotes and foxes and badgers and eagles and ravens and magpies had cleaned it all up. Scarcely a bone was left.

"Well, I won't go hungry," he said to himself, "because I was smart to hang up all those tongues. I will still have a fine feast tonight." But, lo, the mice people had climbed the pole and eaten the meat out of all the tongues, leaving only the outside skin. So Old Man was as hungry as ever. Un-Yuh—that is all.

Napi was a sage, a prankster and an impulsive storyteller. Sometimes he did good deeds, and at other times he was malicious. He could be kind or cruel, vulgar and obscene or well-mannered and very moral.

There are many well-known traditional tales of Napi that are repeated over and over with slight variations, but an imaginative storyteller could invent tales of his own that were every bit as good as the originals. Napi stories of the Blackfeet are endless and include all subjects, some of great interest to the young, and others reserved for the enjoyment of adults only. At any rate, when the evenings were long, youngsters would constantly badger the old ones with, "Grandfather, tell us another story of Napi." Grandfather would oblige with fantasies kept alive by a vivid imagination and the hypnotic lights of the lodge fire. Night after night Grandfather would spin tales of Napi.

According to The People, Napi (Old Man) made all things. He came from somewhere to the south of Blackfeet country traveling ever northward, creating all living things that are now in the air, on the earth and in the water. He would make rivers, lakes and mountains any time and any place he wished. He made Man out of river clay, and then to give him some company, Napi formed Woman.

Now in these early, wondrous days, all living creatures could speak to each other so Napi invited all to a big council to decide where they wanted to live. Some wanted the mountains so they could climb and jump; others wanted the plains where they could run and play; still others wanted to live in the water; and some rare ones even wanted to fly in the air.

When Man was asked where he wanted to live, he became very eager and said that not only did he want to live where all the other creatures lived, but he also wanted to keep on living and never die. Napi slyly gave Man several challenges saying that if he could catch one of each of the different creatures with his hands, he could have his wish to live anywhere. But as to the matter of never having to die, Napi said he would have to arrange another test.

Man went on his quest and in due time returned with one of each of all the creatures except the ones that lived in the air. None of these could he capture. Man could now live in the mountains, on the plains and swim in the water, but he could not fly like the birds. Then he want to Napi and asked to try the "live forever" test. Woman spoke up and said to Napi, "Will we be here always—with no end? Please—let *me* take the test."

Whereupon Napi took them to the river and told the woman to choose between two things: a dry buffalo chip or a rock. When she had chosen, he said, "Woman, you will now find out whether you go on forever or whether there will be an end to living. One of these things will float and the other will sink. If you chose the floating one, you will live forever, but if you chose the one that sinks, there will be an end to all living things. Now throw it as far as you can into the river."

Woman made a mighty throw with the rock because she thought the heavier object was much the better and would go farther out into the water. But, alas, it sank. "All right," Napi said, "you have picked the sinking one. You thought it of more value because it was heavy, foolish Woman. From now on, there will be an end to all things that live. OKI (pronounced Oak-yuh)." This is a Blackfeet myth of how The People became mortal.

Illustrated in this sculpture is one such tale of how Napi taught the animals of the Beaver Bundle to do their dance. Beaver sings and beats time with rattles on a dry buffalo rawhide spread on the ground. Lynx sits in the foreground because he is a very important part of the ceremony. Sinopah (Fox) is important enough to have a society named after him. Miscinskee (Badger) is so sacred to the Blackfeet that the holiest of all bundles, the Natoas Bundle of the Holy Woman, is wrapped in his skin.

Otter is clever and a clown among animals; he has many lodges painted in his honor. White Weasel is connected with all things Holy, but because his long tail would get in the way while dancing, he sent his cousin, Mink, to learn the dance. Muskrat is very important because he is the one who brought up mud from the waters that covered the world and gave it to Napi so that he could make the ground. Rabbit is respected for his speed and fertility and Skunk for his independent attitude. Several clans are named in Skunk's honor. The Mice People are everywhere present, so naturally they too attend the dance. Napi, as generally imagined, is a short-legged, large-headed, gnomish, pot-bellied character as he is portrayed in this sculpture.

SYMBOLISM

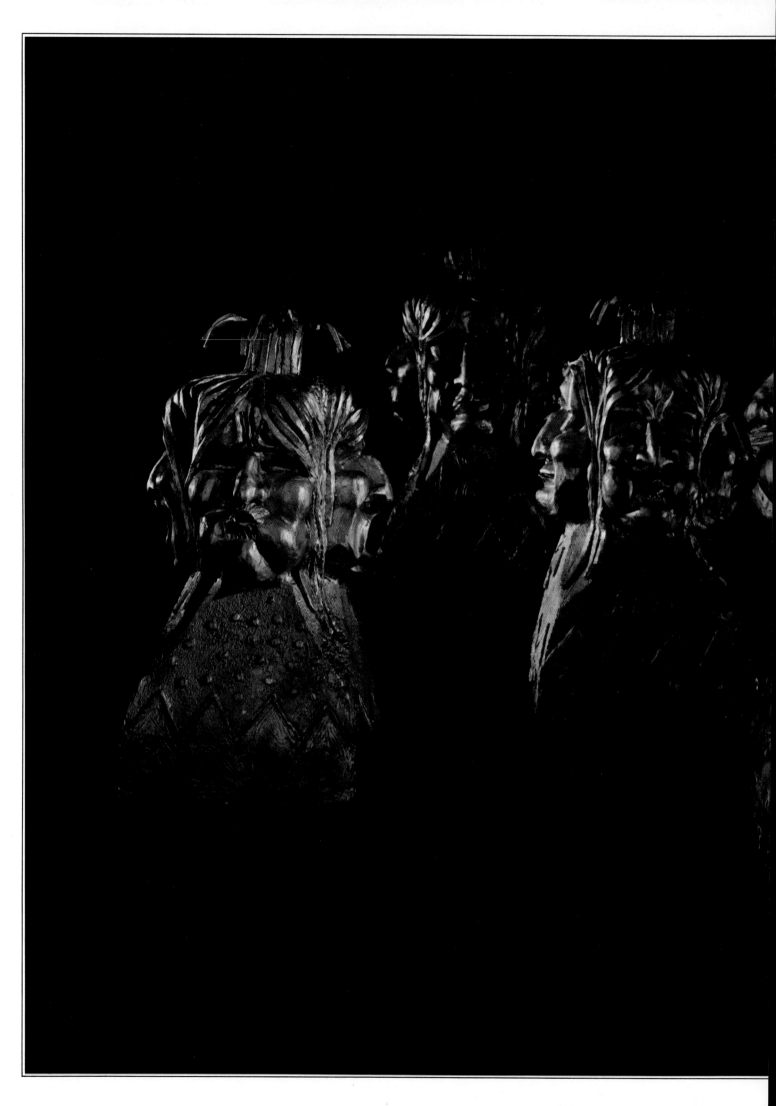

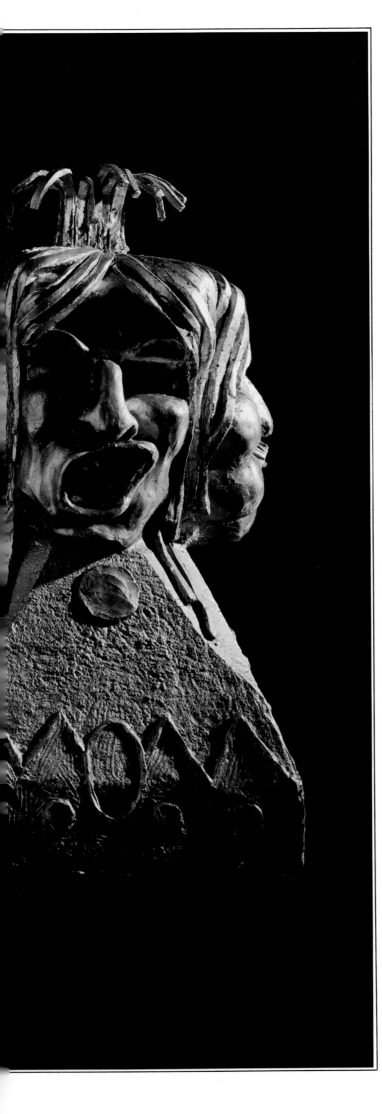

FOUR WINDS

This piece, a four-sided figure based upon basic Blackfeet tipi designs, combined with a stylized rendition of my concept of the Four Directions or the Four Winds, evolved from a tiny model that was to serve as a bronze gavel head to be presented to Secretary of the Interior Harold Ickes upon his visit to the Blackfeet. The original version, about two inches high, was flat on both ends so as to serve as a gavel once a handle had been attached. This project never materialized and so was abandoned.

I kept the small clay version, however, and when I was searching for ideas for this series, I thought that this tiny model might have possibilities. It looked as though it might adapt itself to a more imposing treatment so I made a sculpture of it in its present size. Using a pyramidal form to represent the shape of a tipi and suggesting the basic four pole structure of a Blackfeet lodge, I have added stylized interpretations of the faces of the Four Winds. Around the bottom on all four sides are shown the traditional mountain peak design together with circles representing lakes or "fallen stars"—the Blackfeet term for puff balls.

Blackfeet tipis always face the east, so the side representing East has a doorway and the Sun sign. The stylized face is that of a camp crier greeting the rising Sun and awakening the camp with instructions for the day. As a boy I can remember old Mountain Chief doing just that in a voice that could be heard all over town. He needed no mechanical means to make himself heard; his was a powerful voice!

The south side of the design is decorated with rain and lightning symbols. The face is that of South Wind which brings warm rains, chinook winds and the green growth of the new prairie grass.

The west side is decorated with what is known as the Dream Moth that is present on the west side of all Blackfeet dream-painted lodges. West Wind is shown having a pleasant dream. He is very important because he blows the rains away in summer and keeps the prairie free of snow in winter.

The north side is decorated with the snow design and depicts Cold Maker blowing a blizzard down from the Arctic. He is much feared because his is a breath of the season when animals and men can freeze to death.

The entire sculpture is topped with a stylization of the nineteen- and seventeen-pole construction of a Blackfeet lodge.

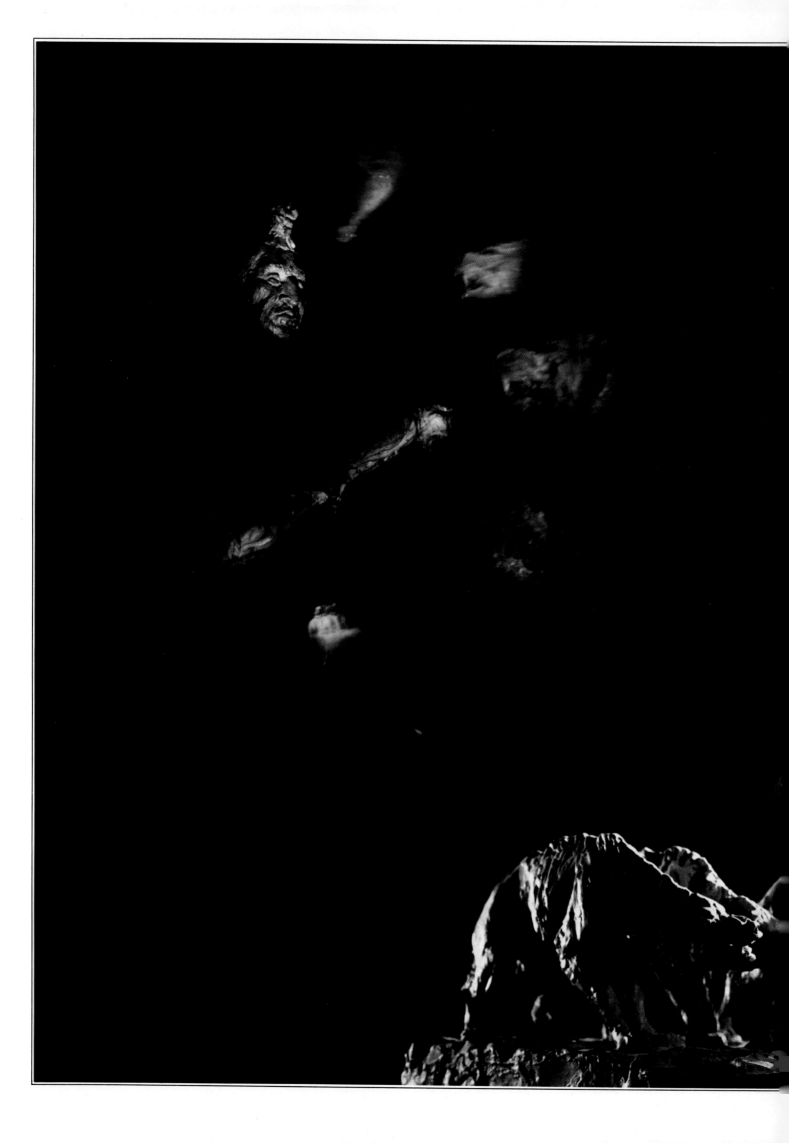

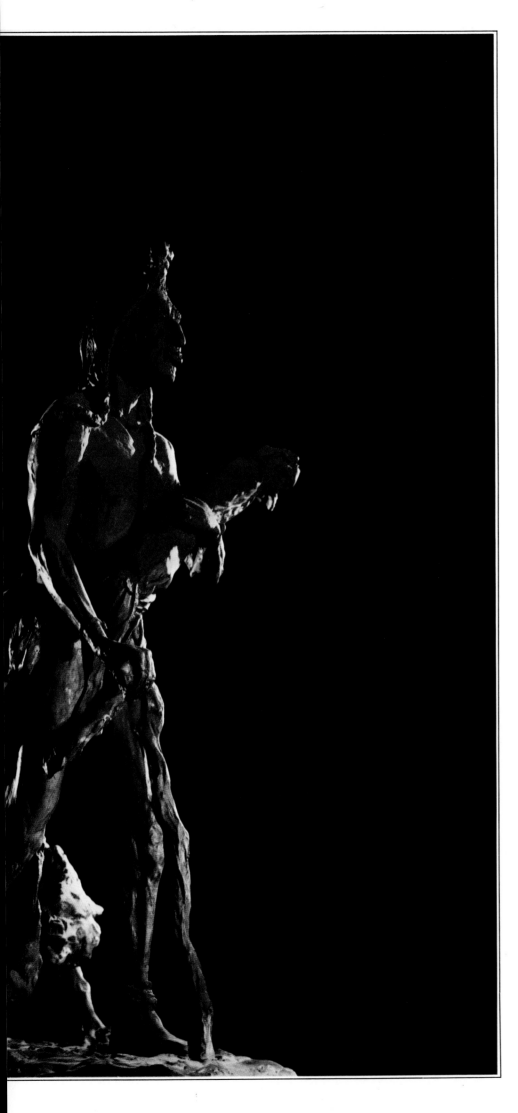

LET THE CURS YAP!

The People of the long, long ago had little in the manner of religious concepts; but as their civilization matured, their ways changed, and legends and moral beliefs developed. Living with nature as they did, all things became objects of strength and guidance. Legend has it that the Beaver Bundle was developed first and hence is the oldest. While it was a very important and prestigious Bundle, it came about that the Pipe given to The People by Thunder grew to become more powerful and therefore much sought after.

The People believed in the Pipe and the Power that Thunder had told them was theirs. It protected them from all sorts of evil, both in peace and in war, and it gave them long life and good health. A person might argue that the Pipe stem has no Power, really. In a way this is true for it is merely a long piece of wood with a hole burned down the center, decorated with plumes, beads, hawk bells, pieces of ribbon and strips of white weasel fur. Twelve feathers from a war eagle's tail formed in a fan shape are suspended at one end of the stem. This entire assemblage is wrapped in several layers of calico and placed in an open-ended, sleeve-like carrying case made from red or black stroud trade cloth.

But any object has religious significance and power when people give it Significance and Power; when they have faith that an object has Power, then most assuredly it is powerful. That is the way it is with the Medicine Pipe!

Perhaps the reason why the Pipe was called upon for help more often than the Beaver Bundle was because it could be easily carried. The Pipe stem, wherein lies the

Power, is comparatively small. Therefore it could be taken on personal pilgrimages and even carried to war. Its Power is called on even to this day, whereas the Beaver Bundle, as a major religious influence, is virtually extinct.

This sculpture shows a Medicine Pipe Man as he strides through an enemy camp protected by the Power of the Holy Pipe he is carrying. Wolf dogs snarl and snap at his heels, but they fear to attack him. Head erect, he ignores them and moves on directly toward the lodge of the enemy chief, secure in his faith that the Power of the Holy Pipe he carries will protect him.

A Pipe owner was treated with great respect by all of the tribes of the Great Plains. He was considered a Holy Man and, as such, was granted rights and privileges that were not accorded to the average person.

This discussion so far has been about the Power of the Pipe and the belief of The People in that Power, but as I considered a title for the piece, "Let the Curs Yap!" suggested itself. The Pipe Man, in ignoring the three snarling dogs, proved that his faith would not let them harm him.

So, I would like to propose that this sculpture shows that we in today's world can have a parallel to this Power. If we can muster the faith to persevere in the face of adversity—our "curs" being greed, disappointment, poor health, fire, flood and the I.R.S.—disregarding these as the Pipe Man ignores the vicious camp curs, we will develop a stronger, more resilient character. As the Pipe Man mastered his life, we also can be the masters of our own lives.

No More Buffalo

The cliffs where the bison drives occurred in days of the long ago have always intrigued me. I have seen the long rows of piled rocks, now sunken in the sod, extending a mile or more in a great V, ever narrowing until the apex ended at the jumping-off place. I have picked up arrow and spear points and have seen layers of buffalo bones ten feet thick exposed by erosion at the base of these cliffs. I have dreamt of what it must have been like to stand on the brow of a high hill overlooking the plains dotted with the great round-backed wild cattle.

One day I observed an elderly Blackfeet who had all the characteristics of what to me was the typical Plains Indian: tall, lithe, with the noble bearing of a proud person. He had the distinctive full hawk-like nose and piercing eyes of a far-seeing prairie person. I ap-

proached him and asked if he would come with me and pose for a piece of sculpture I had in mind. He agreed, so we went to my studio where I got out some clay and started to make some quick sketches. After learning that his name was Ed Big Beaver, I explained to him what I had in mind. "Eddy," I said, "I want to portray an old-time Blackfeet with only a spear for his weapon, dressed in moccasins, breechcloth, belt and knife. No feathers or other props will we use. This man is standing on a high and windy hill near the Two Medicine River buffalo jump cliffs looking off across the plains that once were dotted with buffalo but are silent and empty now. He realizes that with the passing of the buffalo, so too will there be the passing of his kind."

He struck a position right off and said, "How's this?" It was just what I had wanted. Hopefully, I caught the pose and, more importantly, the feeling. I named the piece "No More Buffalo" and have used it as the title piece for this series because I feel that it symbolically tells the whole poignant story of the end of the free old-time Neetsee-tahpee (The People) in one simple, yet powerful, statement.

Interestingly, as soon as I had explained the concept of the piece to Eddy, he struck the pose I wanted as if he were a professional. His reply, casually made, was that he indeed had posed for other sculptors in his younger days. Among them was a sculptor by the name of Phimister Proctor!

Eddy Big Beaver approved the clay model but never lived to see the finished bronze statue of "No More Buffalo." He was found robbed and beaten to death in a ditch near Seattle, Washington. I hope he would approve of the statue as his family comes to my studio occasionally to see the bronze of "Grandpa."

Life's Stream

In this series about the Blackfeet I had modeled only one piece involving the all-important buffalo and then only in a scene of mounted hunters on a chase. Since every part of the animal was used, I considered it especially important to show somehow that the buffalo was inextricably linked to the lives of The People. It provided them with almost all of their daily needs of food, shelter and clothing.

Not only did the buffalo provide for their physical needs, but a great many of their religious functions and rituals were based on it: Mototik, the buffalo women's society; Iniskum, the sacred buffalo stone; buffalo horn headdresses; buffalo songs in Medicine Pipe ceremo-

nies; the calling of the buffalo in the Beaver ceremony; the cutting of the hide to tie the Sun Lodge together; and the one hundred sacred tongues sacrament were only a few of the ways the buffalo was involved or incorporated into their religious functions.

The country where The People lived was one of the finest areas on the continent for big game. From the rugged mountain peaks to far out on the prairie many species of animals were to be found. The climate was often harsh and unpredictable, but not unbearable. The prevailing winds from the west were strong, but they cleared the skies and swept the snow from the hills in winter and moved the great rain clouds over the prairie in summer. This was the kind of country and climate that was ideally suited for the great herds of buffalo.

In this sculpture I have used ovals encased in a pyramid as the basic design. The ovals formed in the ancient sign of infinity ∞ tend to give the feeling of continuity, while the pyramid suggests the stability of this evolving life process.

The buffalo calf represents the future of its species while the young Blackfeet mother and child symbolize the parallel concept that in the female and young lie the future of The People. Although the sculpture is realistic in nature, I have tried to show a much deeper significance than merely a buffalo calf, a mother and a child. Here is the continuance of both species, as it were, each dependent on the other.

TRANSITION

At first glance, this piece suggests a family group. However, there is a much deeper meaning intended: to show in one powerful, monumental-style sculpture the transition of a race of people from one culture to another. To emphasize solidarity, I employed the pyramid as the basic design for the grouping of the figures, consisting of an old man, a middle-aged woman and a young boy.

I consider myself very fortunate in having lived during this period of Blackfeet history and having been an on-the-scene observer of this transition. The old ones of the buffalo days like Mountain Chief, Lazy Boy, Green-Grass-Bull, Two Guns-White Calf, Turtle, Chewing Black Bone, Shoots First and all the others are now gone. They were unilingual and unicultural and held fast to their traditional beliefs. Their names were not preceded by a "first" name.

Their progeny and others that came after them were bilingual and bicultural. They kept Blackfeet family names but added a "first" name, as in Jim White Calf, Joe Turtle, John Mountain Chief, Aaron Shoots First. They were knowledgeable in both cultures—the old and the new.

Then came the young people of today, who are mostly unilingual and unicultural (that culture being Anglo-American). Their

family names, too, have become anglicized with a few exceptions. We now have Kipp, Monroe, Clark, Murphy, Lewis along with Mountain Chief, Skunkcap, Old Person.

Efforts are being made in Reservation public schools to help recapture the lost culture of The People. This is commendable but all the same, the buffalo are gone, the land is fenced and the rules and regulations of "civilization" are here; the very reasons that gave rise to their ancient culture have ceased to exist. These young students gain only a superficial knowledge of their culture and a bare smattering of their native language which is very difficult to master with some words being nearly impossible to pronounce on a tongue educated in English. Knowledge of the old ways is gained largely by referring to books written in English by Catlin, Schultz, Wissler, McClintock, Ewers and others, all Anglo-Americans.

Human cultures exist where there is need—change the need or reason for a culture, and it soon ceases to exist. All cultures are in a constant state of flux, and once a certain stage of development is passed, it can not be recaptured.

In order to create this sculpture with accuracy, I had to find models who actually were the kinds of people I wanted to portray. The old Indian must have lived in the buffalo days, must look typically Blackfeet and be willing to pose for his portrait. Chewing Black Bone was such a person, so it was he whom I chose for that part. A venerable ninety-six years old, he had chased and killed wild buffalo, had taken an enemy scalp at the age of fourteen and believed in Sun's Power and paid homage to Him in daily prayers. He spoke fluently but only in Blackfeet.

At first, Chewing Black Bone was unwilling to pose, but through the pleadings of a mutual friend, he and his family finally gave consent. Pride and regal bearing were evident in his every move as he sat in his lodge, and I worked to capture his physical and intrinsic image. He was totally blind at the time he sat for me, yet I knew that he approved after he had run his hands ever so lightly over the finished clay model. I had brought him some goods, fruit and other presents, but the gift that pleased him most was a beautiful center feather from a war eagle's tail.

I have shown him head bowed and reflecting on past glories, dressed only in breechcloth, buckskin leggings and moccasins. His hair is done up in the traditional Blackfeet three-braid manner. His smoking pipe, tobacco bag and cutting board are near. No feathers or other props are needed to show that here sits a real Blackfeet.

The woman figure, the most prominent of the three, is shown as the transitional person, the connecting link between the old and the new. The model, Many Victories Women (Mae Williamson), was the official interpreter for her tribe for many years. Raised in the Indian way, she as a young girl was sent to a Catholic mission school to learn the white ways and so became bicultural and bilingual, extremely conversant in either language as the occasion demanded. An influential figure for good, she was able to see in true perspective the changing world of her people.

Many Victories Woman is symbolic of the transition that is taking place. Four hundred matched pairs of elk tusks adorn her elk-skin dress, her hair is neatly braided in the traditional two braids for women and moccasins are on her feet. Her hand gently touches the past in the person of Chewing Black Bone, but she looks intently into the face of the young boy as her arm protectively shelters him. She knows that the hope for her people lies in the young.

The young boy, whose name I know not, will remain anonymous. He gazes inquiringly into the eyes of the woman, sensing these things. He speaks only English, wears a white shirt and pressed trousers and has shoes on his feet. A schoolbook is under his arm, and a comb for his hair that is shorn of braids rests in his pocket. In him lies the future of his people. He is learning the new ways and is learning to cope with today's world. The old ways are gone but not the Spirit—The People will survive.

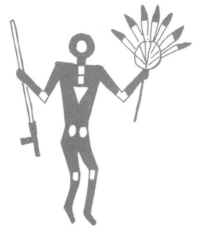

LEGENDS OF
THE BLACKFEET

LEGENDS OF THE BLACKFEET

In doing this series of sculptures, I have used several interpretive styles in attempting to find the best way to depict each piece. Some of them were best modeled realistically as in "Trade Goods," while others, such as "A Warrior's Vow," were better treated in an impressionistic manner.

One piece, however, became wholly abstract. It came about in the following manner. Having gotten deeply involved not only in the material culture of The People but also in their religious beliefs I found myself contemplating more and more the ethereal aspects of their lives. In this series, I had made figures of humans, animals and birds, in both realistic and impressionistic styles. But as I held a small piece of clay in my hands one evening and was just doodling while thinking of the Power of the Pipe and the presence of The People all around me, the miniature of this abstraction commenced to take form.

Ah ha!, I thought, the *outline* of the object was not the important thing this time! The piece was to be an inside-out sculpture. By way of explanation I mean that in the average sculpture the *outline* is what defines

the object, but in this piece the *indentations* and *apertures* were to give it substance and meaning. The excitement became intense as my hands and mind eagerly searched for inner meanings, and I became aware of a deeply moving experience. It was a sculptural object that had never before existed, and it was inspired by my feeling for this magnificent people, their beliefs, their dreams.

In a manner of speaking, this abstraction has been the most difficult of all because there were no guidelines such as there are when one models some recognizable object. I wanted it to be purely an imaginary concept, and so any identifiable shape that materialized was immediately eliminated.

This piece is designed to revolve on a pedestal, and as it turns slowly (as shown in this photograph by Marshall Noice) the indentations and projections lead the eye upward level by level to the highest pinnacle where Sun's rays illuminate the inner cavern recesses from the top. Voices of a beautiful tribal hymn emanate from somewhere deep inside. Fire glows from the caverns near the bottom of the sculpture and symbolizes man's first control over his environment. I hope this becomes an interesting piece to contemplate.

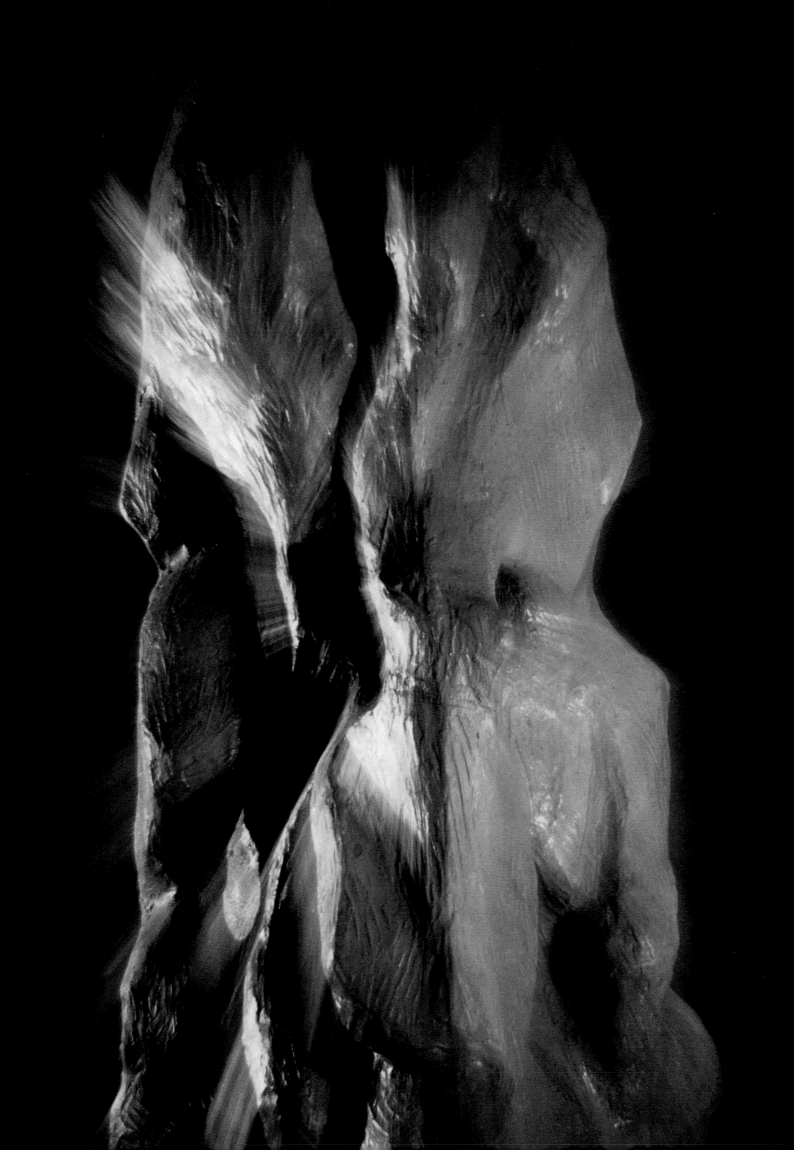

A WORD ABOUT THE SCULPTURE

As noted previously, there were several basic sculptural methods used. A piece could either be illustrative (where the primary concern is an illustration of an incident with design and composition being of secondary importance); impressionistic (whereby the story is told with a minimum of detail, leaving the viewer much latitude in his interpretation); symbolic (in which the piece has a hidden deeper meaning that is not apparent at first glance); or abstract as in "Legends of the Blackfeet."

On the facing page, Nicholas deVore III has shown this piece as giving off cosmic forces emanating from its human and animal forms that are held together in a common bond of mutual dependency which is the basis of all life on this planet.

On the following page, I have listed the title, date of copyright, size and major exhibits of all the foregoing sculptures. The date of copyright does not necessarily coincide with the date I actually sculptured the piece because some of the ideas were conceived twenty years ago but lay dormant as merely quick clay sketches.

Regarding surface treatment, I have used all the way from finely drawn detail to mere suggestions of what I wanted to portray.

An artist must perceive and get to the essence of that which he wishes to portray. Of course, proportions and anatomy must be basically correct, but good art must go beyond that. It must be an emotional experience for the viewer and sculptor alike—however, this experience need not be the same for everyone.—R.M.S.

THE ILLUSTRATIONS

Title	Copyright Year	Dimensions (height x width x length	Major Exhibitions*
At the Beginning	1978	42 x 15 x 17	
Before the Horse	1978	33½ x 21½ x 44	
The Way It Was	1978	18½ x 12¼ x 18½	CAA
Coming of Elk-Dog	1978	33 x 26 x 41	NAWA
The First Horse	1978	10¼ x 13 x 21	
A Warrior's Prize	1978	15 x 12½ x 14½	
★ Grandfather Tells of the Horse	1978	14 x 13½ x 22	Gold Medal/CAA
The Buffalo Decoy	1978	15 x 9 x 7	CAA
The Buffalo Horse	1978	13½ x 10 x 15	CAA
Real Meat	1964	14 x 28 x 30	BBMC/WGWA
★ The Buffalo Runner	1967	11¼ x 14 x 26½	Monaco, Gold Medal/CAA
Yellow Wolf, Setter of Snares	1978	10½ x 12 x 21	
The Hide Scraper	1978	8½ x 7 x 10	
Firewood	1978	17 x 10 x 7	
Blackfeet Family Portrait			
Napi	1978	24½ x 18 x 11	
Kip-Ah-Talk-Ee	1978	23½ x 16½ x 10	
White Quiver	1978	22 x 19½ x 11	Peking, Paris, NAWA
Pitamakin	1978	22 x 16 x 10	
Timmy	1978	15 x 12 x 9	
Three Courtship Scenes			
At The Spring	1978	11½ x 12½ x 10½	CAA
Prairie Romance	1978	9½ x 15½ x 12	CAA
The Proposal	1978	13 x 17 x 11	CAA
Owner of the Lodge	1978	18 x 10¼ x 24	CAA
Hand Game	1978	14½ x 13 x 27	
Waiting for the Dance	1978	20½ x 6 x 6	
Dance Contest	1978	24 x 24 x 40	
Little Brother Goes Swimming	1978	11¼ x 4½ x 15	CAA
The Horse Race	1978	9 x 8½ x 15	
Parade Indian	1978	20 x 6 x 16½	MHS
Return of the Blackfeet Raiders	1960	15 x 19 x 25	BBMC/WGWA, MHS
Standing Alone	1978	19½ x 8 x 5	

Title	Copyright Year	Dimensions (height x width x length)	Major Exhibitions*
Winter Scouts	1978	16½ x 12 x 19	NAWA
Straight-Up Bonnet with Boss Ribs	1978	32 x 13 x 15	
The Split Horn Bonnet	1978	16½ x 9½ x 8	CAA
Enemy Tracks	1963	13 x 10 x 16	BBMC/WGWA
The Fast Blanket	1978	18 x 8 x 9	
The Price of a Scalp	1963	15 x 12 x 9½	BBMC/WGWA
To Take a Scalp	1978	13 x 11 x 20	CAA
War Pony	1978	13 x 5½ x 13	
End of the War Trail	1978	32½ x 31 x 29½	
He-That-Looks-At-The-Calf Meets Captain Lewis	1978	15½ x 24 x 48	
Trade Goods	1978	12½ x 14 x 18	
Onesta and the Sacred Bear Spear	1978	24½ x 9 x 7½	
The Holy Woman	1978	22 x 11 x 45	
A Warrior's Vow	1978	26½ x 18½ x 20½	NAWA
Opening of the Thunder Medicine Pipe	1969	19 x 55 x 55	BBMC/WGWA
Dance of the Beaver Women	1978	16½ x 55 x 55	
The Story of Miscinskee	1978	26 x 17 x 28	
Tailfeathers Woman and Morning Star/Scarface	1978	34½ x 26 x 33	
The Raven Speaks	1978	24 x 19 x 28	
The Beaver Lover	1978	17 x 22 x 18	
Secrets of the Night	1978	26 x 17 x 12	
Napi Teaches Them the Dance	1978	16 x 30 x 23	
Four Winds	1978	24 x 12 x 12	
Let the Curs Yap!	1978	21½ x 13 x 26	
No More Buffalo	1957	22 x 6 x 8	GM, BBMC/WGWA
Life's Stream	1978	17 x 12 x 26	
Transition	1960	18 x 11 x 22	GM, BBMC/WGWA
Legends of the Blackfeet	1978	34 x 15½ x 13	

*Many of these sculptures have never before been shown to the public. "The Charles Marion Russell Museum, located at Great Falls, Montana, was selected for this world premiere because of Russell's love for the Blackfeet with whom he lived," said Ray W. Steele, museum director. Russell did many paintings and sculptures of the Blackfeet and was a frequent visitor to Browning, Montana at the annual Indian Days celebration.

CAA—Cowboy Artists of America, Phoenix, Arizona

GM—Glenbow Museum, Calgary, Alberta, Canada

NAWA—National Academy of Western Art, Oklahoma City, Oklahoma

BBMC/WGWA—Buffalo Bill Memorial Center and Whitney Gallery of Western Art, Cody, Wyoming

Monaco—International Art Guild, Palais de la Scala, Monte Carlo, Monaco

MHS—Montana Historical Society, Helena, Montana

BIOGRAPHY

Robert Macfie Scriver was born August 15, 1914, in the Blackfeet Indian Reservation town of Browning, Montana, where he has lived most of his life. Scriver's father came to Montana from Montreal in 1903 and in 1906 became a government-licensed Indian Trader. His store still operates in Browning and is owned and managed by Bob's brother, Harold. Their mother was of aristocratic Scottish ancestry.

As a child, Bob Scriver showed natural artistic talent and was molding small animal figures from mud clay at age seven, but he was never encouraged to take it seriously. "In those days," he explains, "art was frowned upon. It was not considered a 'job.' A man had to pursue a career that would guarantee him a livelihood and be respectable." Scriver went on to college to study to be a music teacher and cornet player, earning both B.M. and M.M. degrees. For seventeen years, he put his love for art out of his mind but was even then busily sketching everyday scenes around Chicago and in the Field Museum. These little quick sketches on 3 x 5' cards show a remarkable feel for line and composition.

While attending the VanderCook College of Music in Chicago, Scriver honed his self-taught skills in taxidermy by, in his words, "making a nuisance of myself to head taxidermist, Leon Walter, of the Field Museum of Natural History (now the Chicago Museum of Natural History). This long-term interest resulted in a vast collection of specimens which he displayed in a wildlife museum connected to his studio for study purposes as well as for everyone's enjoyment. Nearly every species of bird, fish and mammal native to Montana was represented before a fire that nearly destroyed both museum and studio in 1975.

Although Bob Scriver did not take his sculpting seriously until his forty-second year, there is no doubt that the effect of nature surrounding him, his knowledge of anatomy, his ability to compose and create music, and the diverse backgrounds of his parents have been important influences in the life of this man, one of today's greatest sculptors.

In 1956, a contest was announced by the state of Montana to choose the best sculpture of Charles M. Russell, Scriver's lifelong idol. The winning sculpture was to be placed in the Hall of Fame in Washington, D.C. Scriver entered the contest and lost, but it gave him the incentive to pursue his career as a serious sculptor. According to Scriver, "Losing the contest was the best thing to happen to me. I had to try harder." He adds, "And I'm still trying." An interesting footnote to this story is that twenty-three years later he was the sculptor chosen to do the heroic-size statue of C. M. Russell which stands now near the famous cowboy-artist's home and museum in Great Falls, Montana.

"Bob Scriver is the foremost sculptor in America today—bar none," writes Dr. Harold McCracken, Director Emeritus, Whitney Gallery of Western Art, in *An Honest Try.*

Scriver has been accorded gold and silver medals for excellence in sculpture by both the Cowboy Artists of America and the National Academy of Western Art. His work was featured at a one-man show at the prestigious Whitney Gallery of Western Art in Cody, Wyoming, in 1969. June 3, 1972 was proclaimed "Bob Scriver Day" by Montana Governor Thomas Judge. His work won "Best of Show" in sculpture at the C. M. Russell auctions in 1976 and 1977.

Scriver's bronzes, "Opening of the Thunder Medicine Pipe Bundle," "Paywindow" and "Return of the Blackfeet Raiders" appear in the National Geographic books, *The World of the American Indian, The American Cowboy in Life and Legend* and *In the Footsteps of Lewis and*

Clark, respectively. His work is featured in Patricia Broder's *Bronzes of the American West* and has appeared several times in *National Sculpture Review* magazine and the *American Artist* magazine. Bob Scriver was picked as the premiere Montana artist in *National Geographic's* May 1976 issue. He wrote a pictorial essay titled *An Honest Try,* also published by The Lowell Press, to accompany his thirty-three piece Rodeo Series in bronze, which covers the era of rodeo from Bill Linderman to Jim Shoulders. He is a patron of the National High School Rodeo Association, the Official Sculptor of the Pro Rodeo Cowboy Association and executed a heroic size bronze of Rodeo's "King," Bill Linderman. He is commissioned to do a 22-foot high rodeo bronc rider for the Pro Rodeo Hall of Champions at Colorado Springs, Colorado.

Scriver is an interested member in many organizations including the venerable Salmagundi Club in New York, the Blackfeet Holy Medicine Pipe Society, National Sculpture Society, the Society of Animal Artists, International Art Guild (Monaco), the National Academy of Western Art and the Cowboy Artists of America, to name just a few.

Scriver's extensive research and experience has made him one of *National Geographic's* consultants on the Blackfeet and grizzly bears.

Bob Scriver has reached the highest place of honor in his profession, ever pursuing excellence. He vows, "If they took the money out of the art game, there would be few of us left. But I'd do it for the fun of it! As Charlie Russell said, 'Any man that can make a living doing what he likes is lucky'—and I'm that."

THE LODGE OF MISCINSKEE
The Badger Tipi

These pictures show me and my Blackfeet friends putting up the Lodge of Miscinskee (Little Badger). Cecile Mountain Chief Horn is the supervisor—she and her family are among the elite of the Blackfeet since they own a Medicine Pipe Bundle. Cecile and Charlie (now deceased) were attendants at the dedication ceremonies of the Badger tipi. She has made several tipis and is one of the best craftswomen in the old tradition making beautifully beaded moccasins, leggings and shirts.

Twenty-one poles, each twenty-two to twenty-seven feet long, are made from peeled lodgepole pine. Four of the longest poles are tied together with a non-slip knot. A long rope is tied to this knot and with all hands helping, the poles are raised and spread into the basic four-pole position. Fourteen additional poles are then placed on this structure in a certain pattern, leaving one space on the west side for the lodge skin pole. The lodge skin is tied to the fifteenth pole which is then raised and placed in this space. The remaining two poles are for the smoke flaps. The door opening always faces the east. The cover is then wrapped around the poles and laced together with wooden pins. After it is pulled taut, it is pegged down through loops sewn to the bottom edge.

A fire pit, ringed with rocks, is dug in the center of the lodge. The four tipi liners, each made of strips about four feet wide and twelve feet long, are tied to the poles inside the lodge and are anchored at the bottom by rocks. These rings of rocks, left behind when camp was moved, create the famous tipi rings found throughout Indian country.

The two tipis shown here are the Otter tipi and the Badger tipi. The Otter tipi was once owned by Charlie and Cecile, and, of course, the Badger tipi belongs to me as the story on page 87 will attest. I own all the rights and privileges of the Badger tipi because it was from my dream vision that it came to be. I own the bundle, tipi flag, songs and ceremony that accompany it, none of which can be used by others except with the proper transfer ceremony.

I bought the Otter tipi from the Horn family several years ago. However I do not own any of the rights to the design; I merely own this particular lodge skin. If I were to make a new Otter lodge skin, I would have to get permission from Cecile. In the future she may transfer the rights to me which would be very gratifying.

de Vore

Noice

Cree Medicine

NICHOLAS DE VORE III

During the initial stages of work on this book, I began to search for a photographer who could go beyond mere literal translations of the sculpts. I wanted exciting photos—ones that would add new dimensions to the pieces and interpret them as visual experiences of the Blackfeet as a people and not as sculptured art objects.

Being a photographer for the prestigious *National Geographic* Magazine as well as many other top-flight national and international publications, Nicholas deVore III was both technically and emotionally well-qualified for this assignment. We were indeed extremely fortunate when he agreed to join our staff for a brief period in October 1980 for his work set the tone and quality for the entire project.

For seven and one-half days he was a human dynamo—taking pictures before dawn and after sunset. My men who helped him called Nick the "Moonlight Photographer" in jest. Our collective hats are off to Nicholas deVore III for setting the visual impact of the book *No More Buffalo* on such a high plane.—R.M.S.

MARSHALL NOICE

Born in North Dakota in 1952, Marshall moved to Kalispell, Montana, with his parents when he was 16. Having sketched with pencil since childhood, he still composes his more important photographs with detailed thumbnail sketches.

One day he chanced to open a book on landscape photography done by Paul Strand, Edward Weston and Ansel Adams, the greats of black-and-white photography. Their work had such an emotional impact on Marshall that from that moment on he wanted to be a photographer, no matter what.

I had several sculpts unfinished at the time Nicholas deVore had to leave on another assignment to Mt. Everest and the Shirpas. Several of these sculpts required skilled darkroom work, and it was then that I found Marshall Noice—a photographer of exceptional technical ability—and the determination and stick-to-it-iveness to bring a difficult assignment to a successful conclusion.

The images in this book credited to his name attest to how well he has succeeded.—R.M.S.

CARL CREE MEDICINE, SR.

Carl was born in 1936 on Badger Creek in the Blackfeet Reservation, at the site of the old Reservation Agency of 1876. His grandfather was one of the signers of the Treaty of 1888 between the Blackfeet and the U.S. Government, and the name he carries is an old and honored one among the Blackfeet. He is steeped in the lore of his ancestors and is fluent in his native language as well as in English.

An invaluable assistant to me since 1960, we became close friends and have remained so throughout all these years. Carl is well-versed in every facet of my studio/foundry operation and has a natural feel for things artistic.—R.M.S.

APPENDIX

PISKUN SITES

ALBERTA
According to historians at the Glenbow Museum in Calgary:

Head Smashed In Buffalo Jump—eleven miles west of Fort McCleod (Provincial Park).

Old Women's Buffalo Jump—four miles west of Cayley (Provincial Park).

MONTANA
For the area north of Wyoming, west of Havre, east of the Rockies and south of the Canadian border:

Madison Buffalo Jump State Monument—Bozeman area, south of the Manhattan exit on Interstate 90.

Ulm Pishkun (piskun) State Monument—Great Falls area, eight miles south of Great Falls on Interstate 15, then west approximately 2 miles on a gravel road.

Piskun site on Two Medicine River—Browning area, eleven miles south of Browning on Highway 89, then east on gravel road approximately one mile.

Piskun site on Badger Creek—Browning area, approximately eighteen miles south of Browning, then off the road east approximately two miles where Badger Creek crosses the road.

Blackfeet Boarding School Site—Browning area, six miles north of Browning, take a right turn onto the Boarding School road, then six more miles and take the left fork in the road. This is the site of an archaeological dig conducted by *National Geographic.* The site is near the dairy barns of the Boarding School complex.

BIBLIOGRAPHY

For the serious student of the Blackfeet I suggest the following:

Brasser, Ted. *The Pedigree of the Hugging Bear Tipi.* Scottsdale, Arizona: American Indian Arts and Crafts, 1980.

Catlin, George. *North American Indians.* 2 vols. Edinburgh, Scotland, 1926.

Ewers, Dr. John C. *The Blackfeet: Raiders on the Northwestern Plains.* Norman: University of Oklahoma Press, 1958.

_____. *The Horse in Blackfoot Indian Culture.* Washington, D.C.: Smithsonian Institution, 1955.

_____. *Indians on the Upper Missouri.* Norman: University of Oklahoma Press, 1968.

_____. *Plains Indian Painting.* Stanford, California: Stanford University Press, 1939.

Grinnell, George Bird. *Blackfoot Lodge Tales.* New York: C. Scribner's Sons, 1892.

_____. *The Story of the Indian.* New York: D. Appleton and Company, 1906.

Hungry Wolf, Adolf. *Siksika.* Invermere, British Columbia, Canada: Good Medicine Books, 1979.

_____. *The Blood People.* New York: Harper & Row, Inc., 1977.

Hungry Wolf, Beverly. *The Ways of My Grandmothers.* New York: William Morrow & Company, Inc., 1980.

Kehoe, Dr. Tom. "1967 Boarding School Bison Drive Site," *Plains Anthropologist,* Vol. 12, No. 35.

Linderman, Frank B. *Indian Old-Man Stories.* Illustrated by Charles M. Russell. New York: Blue Ribbon Books, 1920.

_____. *Indian Why Stories.* Illustrated by Charles M. Russell. New York: C. Scribner's Sons, 1915.

McClintock, Walter. *The Old North Trail.* London: Macmillan & Co., Ltd., 1910.

Shaeffer, Claude. *Notes from the Years at the Museum of the Plains Indian,* Browning, Montana.

Schultz, James Willard. *My Life As An Indian.* New York: Doubleday, Page & Company, 1907.

_____. *The Sun God's Children.* Boston: Houghton, Mifflin Company, 1930.

_____. *Running Eagle, The Warrior Woman.* Boston: Houghton, Mifflin Company, 1919.

Scriver, Bob and Werner, Wilbur. *Creation of the Badger Tipi* (available from the Smithsonian Institution and the Montana Historical Society, Helena, Montana).

Thwaites, Reuben Gold. *Original Journals of the Lewis and Clark Expedition.* New York: Arno Press, 1960.

Turner, John Peter. *The North-West Mounted Police.* 2 vols. Ottawa: E. Cloutier, King's Printer, 1950.

Wissler, Clark. *Indians of the Plains.* New York: American Museum of Natural History, 1920.

_____. *Ceremonial Bundles of the Blackfoot Indians.* New York: American Museum of Natural History, 1912.

Wissler and Duval. *Mythology of the Blackfoot Indian.* New York: American Museum of Natural History, 1908.

NO MORE BUFFALO

by Bob Scriver

was designed by David E. Spaw,
photocomposed in Palatino,
and printed on Warren's Flokote Enamel
by
The Lowell Press
115 East 31st Street
Kansas City, Missouri 64108

White Calf	Fancy Jim (Co-Chick-sin)	Horace J. Clark
Big Nose	Big Elk	Tom Kiya
Tearing Lodge	Paul (Pone)	Champagn
Last Buffalo	Good Robe Out	Spearson
Crazy Wolf	Cross Gun	Apache Pete
Curly Bear	Left Hand	Spread Out
Big Brave	Old Doctor	Proud Bull
Four Horns	Many Tail Feathers	Crow Eyes
Skunk-Cap	John Power	Worm
Shortie	Bull Calf	Unlucky
Bear Chief	Jim White Calf	Seal
Wolf Tail	Old Top	Weasel Fat
Four Bears	Rye Grass	Old Thing
Almost A Dog	Crow Chief	Mexican Joe
Bear Chief Number Two	Chief Coward	Little Plume
Heavy Collar	Calf Shield	White Calf Robe
Kicking Woman	Chief All Over	Packing Meat
Cold Feet	Roan Horse Rider	Many White Horse
White Calf Number Two	Big Head	Big Top
Hat Tail	Talked About	Bear's Hand
Red Bird Tail	Thunder	Short Hair Robe Ou[t]
Lazy Man	Bite	Mountain Chief
Running In The Road	Iron Crow	Small Bull
Strangling Wolf	Butterfly	Buffalo Adviser
Running Wolf	Dick (Sah-que-na-mah-ka)	Black Weasel
Dogs' Head	Miller	Blood Person
Heavy Roller	Visitor	Eddie Jack
Shooting Up	Takes A Gun	Anthony
Behind The Ears' Tack	Kys	Joe Shorty
Man Mooring	Sandervice	Billy Kipp
Many Guts	Gardipee	Pound
Running Rabbit	Star	Taking Gun At Night
Chief On The Prairie	Kyo	Buffalo Shape
Pete	John White Calf	Catch One Another
One Horn	Kiyo	Good Stabber
Jack (Ne-toot-Skenah)	Oliver Sanderville	Under Swimmer
Mack	Will Russell	Drags Blanket